PRAISE FOR *EXPENSIVE SENTENCES*

"A few words. Phrases we use every day. They seem so innocent. And yet left un-examined, they cost us dearly, both personally and professionally. In *Expensive Sentences* Jack Quarles shows us how we get in our own way when making decisions—and how to get out of it. Save yourself more grief. Get started reading!"

Robert "Jake" Jacobs – Author, Real-time Strategic Change

"A thoroughly engaging read that will improve your decision making both professionally and personally."

Scott McKeon – Professor of Economics, Stanford University

"This isn't theory; Quarles unpacks the many ways that team thinking goes wrong, and provides instantly useful insight and tools to make better decisions."

David Ruud – President, DTE Power and Industrial

"Just scanning the cover of this book recalled several decisions our team had made in recent months that were probably driven by *Expensive Sentences*. After reading a few chapters, I can see how we went wrong; but I also have tools to avoid the traps of stuck/special/ scarce thinking. This book is easy to read and highly practical, and will save my staff time, money, and heartache in the future."

Pastor Chad Gilligan – Calvary Church Toledo

"*Expensive Sentences* draws a clear picture of those all too familiar phrases that can be costly to businesses and often signal the presence of comfort zones to be avoided."

Roy W Willis – CEO, Propane Education & Research Council

"I love this book! *Expensive Sentences* quickly dispels common business myths with thought-provoking, relevant questions, that when answered honestly will assist leaders in creating actionable plans and achieving bottom line results."

Sheryl Clutter – COO, Convene

"Quarles brings poignant insight into how common, accepted business parlance can be taken as gospel, but lead to really wrong conclusions. You've heard them all and probably used some of them: "We're different..." "This is urgent..." "We're too swamped to deal with that now..." "It's too late to turn back now..." and many more. With each, like a surgeon making an incision, he methodically breaks down both the danger of following these clichés without questioning AND, even better, he gives you practical advice on how to respectfully challenge the orthodoxy. You're going to be hearing the phrase "That's an Expensive Sentence!" more and more.

Jeremy Epstein, Founder of Never Stop Marketing and VP, Sprinklr

"This book has changed the way I listen to my clients...and even myself. *Expensive Sentences* provides pragmatic ways to address the mindset that keeps people stuck in the status quo instead of moving forward."

Sue Funkhouser – Managing Principal, Pinwheel Performance

"After reading *Expensive Sentences* I started to notice how often we encounter these phrases in life. I never realized the impact that they have. Thanks to Jack Quarles we recognize these sentences and know how to deal with them. Don't let your mind be blocked by Expensive Sentences... read this book."

Peep Tomingas – CEO Estonian Purchasing & Supply Chain Assn

"*Expensive Sentences* is a must-read for lean-budgeted entrepreneurs and experienced executives alike."

Mark Greathouse – Managing Director, Mid-Atlantic Angels Corp.

"You will find yourself in this message. Any experienced leader will recognize the pitfalls of *Expensive Sentences*, and will find the book challenging, convicting, and ultimately encouraging. Quarles covers the what, the why, and the how, packing the book with practical wisdom to assess today and make better decisions for tomorrow."

Dale Pyne – CEO, Peacemaker Ministries

"*Expensive Sentences* lays out a clean method to laser focus on the patterns that hold us back. Quarles encourages us that change is not only possible, but easier (and faster) than we think! Thank you for reminding us of the great power in our words."

Kacy Paide – Professional Organizer & Founder, The Inspired Office

"A good business book has to be accessible, memorable and actionable. *Expensive Sentences* hits all three targets. From a single conversation that turned up millions of dollars in waste at his former employer, Jack Quarles has developed a new way of looking not just at the way businesses function, but at the way people in all walks of life communicate. By framing obstacles to progress as '*Expensive Sentences*,' Quarles offers tools to identify, and challenge, defeatist ways of thinking and decision-making. Like any good communicator, Quarles structures his book in a way that clearly maps out his learnings and reinforces his key messages. His subtle, self-deprecating humor and 'keep it simple' format make sure his lessons don't get lost amid business-speak."

Peter Delevett – Director, Intel Capital

"Jack Quarles reveals why it's so common for companies to waste money, time, and attention. The insights in *Expensive Sentences* will help teams avoid waste and get results in every area."

Ian Altman – International Speaker, co-author of Same Side Selling

"Organizational leaders tend to look for large stroke top line gains and bottom line reductions, passing over the persistent middle, where so much more can be done to optimize in both directions. Quarles' *Expensive Sentences* exposes and offers fixes for this significant oversight, along with the sloppy and obstinate decision making frames that prevent leaders and their teams from seeing the problem in the first place. Quarles offers multiple cases from which leaders can compare their own experience and learn vicariously, rather than through their own painful circumstance. If the book was priced in the thousands of dollars and you put what you learn here to work, you would be delighted with your investment."

Mark L. Vincent – CEO, Design Group International

"Jack Quarles shows leaders how to better drive success at home and at work. *Expensive Sentences* is a first-rate practical guide to good decisions and becoming a better decision maker."

Mark McWeeny – CEO, Ruelala.com

"*Expensive Sentences* distills many lessons learned over decades as an executive, investor and entrepreneur into discrete themes that are succinct, compelling and most importantly: actionable. The book delivered numerous "aha" moments as I realized some of the traps I have been blindly falling into - and should have identified sooner. Take the time to read this book but don't stop there, share it with your team. Expensive Sentences is the most insightful and actionable book I have read this year."

David C. Robertson, CPA, CFA – Integris Capital Partners

"In planting a red flag wherever we tend to see a situation as 'special,' Quarles shows us how easy it is to fall into the trap of worshipping sacred cows, losing money and wasting time. *Expensive Sentences* is full of compelling examples written in a super-readable style that will inspire you to change your behavior for the better."

Susan Jung Grant, PhD – Professor of Marketing, Boston University

"*Expensive Sentences* links spending decisions to an organization's broader strategic vision. The author's depth in operations is evident as he connects everyday decisions and practices to the important broader question of inherited culture in an organization. One theme we hear often in our MIT global operations leadership program is the need for revitalizing perspectives within even the most successful companies. *Expensive Sentences* relentlessly challenges assumptions even if they have brought success in the past."

Josh Jacobs – Director of Operations & Partner Integration, MIT

"Quarles boils down decades of buying wisdom into a book that's accessible, enjoyable, practical, and extremely valuable for anyone who wants to get the most for their money, time, and energy. You'll feel like you're back in control after reading this book."

Jeff Gallimore – Co-founder and Principal, Excella Partners

"An outstanding leadership manual, as applicable to change management in general as it is to business operations and sourcing. The readable, relevant anecdotes and the author's conversational style make it a deceptively quick read, as the book concisely presents so many essential concepts: strategy and operations, inertia and drift, sunk costs and persistence, automation and delegation, team cohesion and culture, and more. *Expensive Sentences* is perfect for an office book club… highly accessible and actionable. Applies to every function in the organization."

Doug Pontsler - VP Operations & Sustainability, Owens Corning

"*Expensive Sentences* is about so much more than managing cost… recommended to all leaders seeking better decisions and greater impact."

Brad Phillips - Director, PricewaterhouseCoopers

"*Expensive Sentences* is a must-read for anyone who influences resources at their company. Considering the surplus of time and cost-saving techniques within its pages, reading this book will produce a better ROI on your time than on any other activity right now."

Derek Coburn – Author of Networking Is Not Working

"An enjoyable and worthwhile book that provides straightforward but profound challenges to common presuppositions and imparts effective strategies for any leader, particularly in business."

Mike Hernandez – Dean, Regent University School of Law

"Challenging, insightful, and immediately useful with office-ready tools and conversational starters. As an added benefit, many of the principles in the book are as relevant to home life as they are to work. 'I don't have time to read this book' may be the most Expensive Sentence you tell yourself this year!"

Mark Joseph, CFP, CPA – President, Sentinel Wealth Management

EXPENSIVE
SENTENCES

IDEAPRESS
P U B L I S H I N G

IDEAPRESS PUBLISHING

WE PUBLISH BRILLIANT BUSINESS BOOKS

www.ideapresspublishing.com

All trademarks are the property of their respective companies.

Cover Design by Faceout Studio, Jeff Miller

Interior Layout design by Anton Khodakovsky, BookCoversForAll.com

ISBN: 978-1-940858-25-8   MHID: 1-940858-25-9

Ebook ISBN: 978-1-940858-28-9   MHID: 1-940858-28-3

PROUDLY PRINTED IN THE UNITED STATES OF AMERICA

IdeaPress Books are available at a special discount for bulk purchases
for sales promotions and premiums, or for use in corporate training
programs. Special editions, including personalized covers, a custom
foreword, corporate imprints and bonus content are also available.
For more details, email: *info@ideapresspublishing.com*.

No animals were harmed in the writing, printing or distribution of this book.
The trees, however, were not so lucky.

EXPENSIVE SENTENCES

Debunking the Common Myths that

Derail Decisions and Sabotage Success

JACK QUARLES

CONTENTS

THE SNARE OF CONVENTIONAL WISDOM

"That one may smile, and smile, and be a villain."
—*HAMLET*, ACT 1

"She's like a Milk Dud, Lisa. Sweet on the outside; poison on the inside."
—BART SIMPSON

"It's a trap!"
—ADMIRAL ACKBAR, *STAR WARS EPISODE VI*

ONE OF THE GREAT PLOT DEVICES IS THE TRAP, OR SNARE: WHEN OUR heroes are lured into situations that look right at first, but land them in peril. They had a good plan, but it turns out to have been based on faulty information or a deceptive premise. Sadly, this experience is not limited to fiction. In our own lives, we know the pain of following a promising path only to realize that it has led to a negative outcome. What seemed like a great decision, based on solid reasoning, ended up costing us time, money, opportunities, or more.

Most of us don't face the foul villains of movies and books, but there is an enemy. The enemy is more sly, more subtle, and just as dangerous. Like Bart Simpson's mythical Milk Dud, it is sweet on the outside and poison on the inside. It sounds like wisdom, but it is an Expensive Sentence.

HOW TEAMS MAKE DECISIONS

Over the past two decades, I have guided teams through hundreds of decisions about investing money and time: what to buy, whom to hire, or how to allocate resources. My role has most often been a sourcing or expense management expert, but I have also led this process many times as an executive, CEO coach, consultant, and board member. The groups I have worked with range from multi-billion-dollar corporations to startups to international non-profits.

At a high level, these teams have all sought the same goal: to get the most value for the resources invested. In most cases, the decision-making process started in a similar way, with a statement of the goal, collection of information, and analysis of data related to costs and benefits. But more often than not, at some point the team drifted away from the process. Instead of continuing a disciplined analysis, the decision-makers were drawn toward one particular idea, as if pulled by gravity. It wasn't always the same idea, but each time it had a similar effect of making other considerations shrink, fade, and disappear.

The defining notion was usually a short sentence and often reflected some inside knowledge:

"They're the best in the business."
"It's too late to change directions and try something new."
"We're different—that won't work here."

In other cases, it was a more general proverb:

"You get what you pay for."
"We can't change horses in mid-stream."
"The customer is always right."

This conventional wisdom sounded good. It rang true. It appeared so self-evident that it was difficult to dispute. So without need for further conversation, the decision was finalized. Everyone nodded their heads, shook hands, and walked away feeling satisfied about where things landed.

Were we just taken in by a smiling villain?

THE FIRST EXPENSIVE SENTENCE

My eyes were first opened to Expensive Sentences when I was the Director of Procurement at a national financial services company. My team had noticed a vendor with whom the company spent almost exactly one million dollars every year. I didn't recognize the vendor's name or know what they did, so I asked the Director of Human Resources, who was responsible for the expense.

"That's our background-check company," she said. "They're great, and you don't need to worry about trying to save money there."

"Why's that?" I asked.

"Because they haven't raised our prices in eight years."

Okay.

That sounded good, but at the time I knew nothing about background checks. So I met with the Vice President of Human Resources and asked again about the vendor.

"Oh yeah, we love those guys. And do you know what?"

("What?" I wondered to myself.)

"They haven't raised our prices in eight years!"

Hmm.

Hearing the same words again raised my curiosity. I still didn't know much about background checks or how much they should cost. After I talked with the VP, we agreed to proceed with a sourcing exercise; that is, we would go shopping. We would check the marketplace, talk to some other companies that provided similar services, and find out if we were getting a good value.

I called the account manager at our current vendor to introduce myself and to let him know our plans to investigate other providers.

"I'm not sure why you'd want to talk to other vendors," he said, sounding nonplussed. (Of course, sales reps are not always excited to hear from the Procurement department.)

"We have a great relationship with you guys, and do you know what else?"

(Wait for it....)

"WE HAVEN'T RAISED YOUR PRICES IN EIGHT YEARS!"

I'd love to claim that I smelled big savings at that point, but the truth is that I was still developing my instincts. The Expensive Sentence was slithering past me, but it hadn't bitten me yet.

We moved forward with our process: getting to know the market, identifying other potential vendors, and conducting a formal request for proposal. The more we learned, the more we started to wonder if that eight-year-old pricing was really as great as it sounded.

It wasn't.

In the end, we found a better-quality solution for a price that was less than HALF of our prior rates. Instead of paying one million dollars yearly, we paid under half a million.

VICTORY OR TRAGEDY?

This is the kind of story that procurement guys love. We come in on a white horse, find a better product for the customer, and deliver six- or seven-figure savings. (Someone should have given me a medal!)

But if you take a minute and flip the story around, consider the negative: our company had overpaid by millions of dollars in the prior years. We were with a vendor that—if not deceptive—was at least content to let us lag behind the market in quality and in price. How could that happen? It happened because of a widespread belief that turned out to be highly misleading: that the absence of a price increase meant we were getting a good deal. "They haven't raised our prices in eight years" turned out to be a very Expensive Sentence.

IT'S A TRAP!

The game is rigged. We've inherited a library of proverbs, conventional wisdom, and cookie-cutter advice for life and business. These phrases are often cited, widely accepted… and sometimes right. In the wrong circumstances, they can be toxic.

"A lie that is half-truth is the darkest of all lies."

—ALFRED TENNYSON

Using one adage to cast doubt on others may seem dubious. As does the warning that all generalizations are false (including this sentence). The point is that simple advice is not so simple, and in fact can be rather treacherous. A phrase that is sometimes apt can at other times deceive and mislead. So our first challenge is to identify these words as either friend or foe.

Is a Sentence Expensive or Not?

We can spot an Expensive Sentence by its impact. Expensive Sentences limit information. They end conversations. They create urgency and isolation. They reduce options. They steal choice.

Despite the fact that Expensive Sentences show up in every context with unlimited variations, their message can be distilled into just three words:

- Stuck

- Special

- Scarce

Expensive Sentences tell us that we are stuck, that someone is special, or that something is scarce. We'll explore the full implications and costs of Stuck, Special, and Scarce, and we will study the most common sentences that advance those conditions.

While it's important to understand that Expensive Sentences are symptoms of flawed thinking, we can't stop there because these symptoms do not simply reveal the disease; they also advance it. Such is the power of words that repeating and believing Expensive Sentences can make things worse.

Fortunately, there is another peculiar quality about Scarce/Special/Stuck thinking. It's the rare disease that can be cured by treating the symptoms. When we expose and correct an Expensive Sentence, we get right to the core of the sickness.

Language reflects our beliefs. It is also true that by improving our language, we can change our beliefs.

This is our great opportunity—and the purpose of this book. We can reject the Scarce myths, refuse the Special myths, and escape the Stuck myths that materialize as Expensive Sentences. We can develop ears to hear these lies in disguise, and use tools to expose and correct them.

After you learn the basics, you will find many opportunities to practice this skill. That's certainly what I found after my first Expensive Sentence.

EXPENSIVE SENTENCES EVERYWHERE

My boss chuckled when I told him about the Expensive Sentence. "I think I've heard a few of those around here," he said.

He was right. In fact, after we labeled "Expensive Sentences," they started showing up on nearly every project we tackled.

"The sales guy told me it's the last one they have at this price." (Scarce)

"This is definitely the firm we want to use. They're the best." (Special)

"We need to implement next week." (Stuck)

These pricey phrases were like a rash all over the company.

I started to see my job in a new way. My biggest challenge on any project was likely to be finding and uprooting the Expensive Sentences. If we didn't address the beliefs underlying those sentences, they would trump any analysis and drive our decisions.

This realization turned my professional world upside down. I was, in my own estimation, a rather brilliant young analyst. My spreadsheets were stunning, my cost models were impeccable, and my PowerPoint presentations were logically irrefutable and visually dazzling. Yet all of these tools could be cast aside with just a few words of "wisdom" that might be misapplied and wildly misleading. Like Superman next to kryptonite, my powers vanished in the face of Expensive Sentences.

I decided to learn the new skill of combatting Expensive Sentences. I began to have some success at the large company I worked for. Later I moved on and began consulting for smaller companies. It was then that I saw even more vividly the need to expose and defeat Expensive Sentences.

A Cost Beyond Money

One of my clients was a forty-person construction company. As we were reviewing the company's expenses, I noticed that the figure for insurance was larger than I expected. When I asked the CEO, he said, "I think we're fine there. Our insurance agent is a good friend—he's been working with us for twenty years. We trust him."

And then he caught himself: "Wait. Did I just say one of your Expensive Sentences?"

My reply was that I wasn't sure, but he just may have said three or four. We decided to find out. We scoped the marketplace and talked to numerous brokers and carriers. What we found was that the company was overpaying by 40 percent based on competitive rates. We made a change and the savings began.

Of course, any project that delivers true savings is beneficial. But there was more to the story with this construction company. The region was still in the wake of a market downturn that had hit the company hard. The prior year the company had to let go several employees to reduce payroll expenses, so it was easy to see how every dollar mattered. In fact, the 40 percent that we saved on insurance covered the salary for two full-time employees.

The trusted insurance broker was not malicious, but perhaps he was negligent. In any event, correcting the Expensive Sentence saved two people their jobs.

Is it possible that Expensive Sentences are affecting the people and organizations you care about?

Is This Book for You?

I am convinced that Expensive Sentences are silently sabotaging companies, non-profits, schools, families, churches, teams, governments, and individuals. Wherever decisions are made and humans are involved, Expensive Sentences threaten.

If you want to make better decisions, this book will help. Since the context for many decisions is the stewardship of money, time, and other resources, we will unpack the key factors that should guide our thinking in these areas:

- Total cost

- The cost (and value) of time

- The cost (and value) of opportunity

- The cost of risk

Though these costs underlie virtually every decision we make, they are widely overlooked and misunderstood. We'll review tools and tactics that lead to a clear understanding of both costs and benefits.

But there is more here than economics. Expensive Sentences have a much higher cost, well expressed in the words of Oliver Wendell Holmes:

The greatest tragedy in America is not the destruction of our natural resources, though that tragedy is great. The truly great tragedy is the destruction of our human resources by our failure to fully utilize our abilities, which means that most men and women go to their graves with their music still in them.

We cannot quantify the damage of sentences that limit potential. The cost of Expensive Sentences transcends the income statement; it affects lives all around us.

What may be surprising is how simple it can be to cut through the biases and assumptions to make better decisions on solid ground, once you're armed with the right insight and tools.

Let's begin.

PART 1

ESCAPING THE
STUCK MYTHS

Expensive Sentences pollute our thinking in different ways. The Scarce myths tell us that there is not enough of something we need or want. The Special myths tell us that someone is outside the rules and principles that apply to others.

The Stuck myths are often the most damaging of all. They tell us that we can't do certain things and that we dare not even think about other things. They deny possibilities. We are robbed of business opportunities, unable to improve relationships, and condemned to unfortunate circumstances – like an animal in a cage.

A cage may present a real constraint, but the Stuck myths present false constraints. If we don't recognize these Expensive Sentences and correct them, however, they can have just as much power as if they were real. We can fall victim to being stuck even when we have freedom and more options than we realize.

We are blessed today with more options than any generation before us: in career choices, in where we live, in entertainment, in what we read, in how we communicate, in the food we eat, and much more. The only thing we don't have more of is time… and perhaps that is why time is central to the most pervasive myths of being stuck. We'll look closely at these three:

- "It's too late to turn back now."

- "We're too swamped to look at that now."

- "We need it yesterday."

"It's too late to turn back now" mixes persistence and momentum with fear of change to tell us that altering our course is not viable. It implies that decisions from the past will drive our future.

"We're too swamped to look at that now" plays upon our time famine and perceived busyness to prevent us from even considering things that might improve our future.

"We need it yesterday" is an acceptance of urgency that hastens decisions and eliminates any options that may take more time.

None of us would willingly give up options that might improve our circumstances. Yet our history, our past relationships, and Expensive Sentences team up to create ceilings on how high we can rise and walls that limit our movements. In this section we'll learn how to see those false ceilings and walls for what they are, both in your life and on your team.

That means that the next time you feel stuck, you may find you have more options than you thought.

CHAPTER 1

"IT'S TOO LATE TO TURN BACK NOW"

*"We've spent too much money
and time on this to let it go."*

"I made a decision; I'm sticking with it."

*"I've been in this field for twenty years;
I can't change careers now."*

"We can't go back."

AS CANDLES THREW FLICKERING SHADOWS AGAINST THE TENT, THE weary generals traded complaints:

> "The army has already diminished by one third, through desertion, famine, and disease. If supplies are scarce here, what will it be like farther on?"
>
> "If we extend any further, the enemy will have in their favor our long drawn-out flank, and their terrible winter."

The room grew silent as all awaited the reply of one man. He was the shortest person in the room, but commanded the reverence of the others. He pronounced clearly, "We shall continue. How can we stop now on the road to glory? It's too late to turn back now!" [1]

It was a daring venture. Napoleon was provoked by a Russian invasion into Polish lands, and he responded by taking the battle to Russia:

> Thus let us go ahead; let us pass Neman River, carry the war on its territory. The second war of Poland will be glorious with the French Armies like the first one.

The celebrated general had good reason for confidence. His boldness and perseverance had served him well and brought victories for his country. Yet the foray into Russia in 1812 would not only signal the downfall of Napoleon's Empire, but would gain infamy as the greatest military disaster in history. Half a century after the march, a French engineer named Charles Minard created a visual depiction illustrating the distance and direction traveled, the temperature, and the number of soldiers. In the original chart, each millimeter represented ten thousand men.

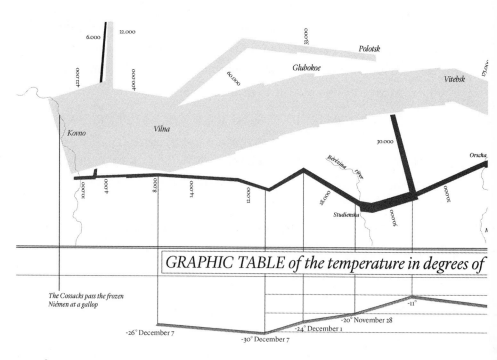

FIGURATIVE MAP of the successive losses in men of the French Army in the RUSSIAN CAM

Drawn by Mr. Minard, Inspector General of Bridges and Roads in retirement. Paris, 20 November 1869. The numbers of men present are represented by the widths of the co men; these are also written beside the zones. Red designates men moving into Russia, black those on retreat. — The informations used for drawing the map were taken from Chambray and the unpublished diary of Jacob, pharmacist of the Army since 28 October. In order to facilitate the judgement of the eye regarding the diminution of the arm under Marshal Davoust, who were sent to Minsk and Mobilow and who rejoined near Orscha and Witebsk, had always marched w

6.000
22.000
33.000
Polotsk
Glubokoe
60.000
Vitebsk
Kovno
Vilna
30.000
Orscha
Bérésina river
30.000
8.000
14.000
12.000
28.000
Studienska
50.000

GRAPHIC TABLE of the temperature in degrees of

The Cossacks pass the frozen Niémen at a gallop

-11°
-20° November 28
-24° December 1
-26° December 7
-30° December 7

The shaded area at the left of the chart is thick, representing well over 400,000 French soldiers. As the upper stripe moves to the right—signifying the march to Moscow—the thinning band reflects the number of men lost to disease, starvation, battle casualties, and desertion. In the trek to Moscow, Minard's numbers show that the army lost over 300,000 men—leaving less than one-fourth of the original number. The march home was also merciless; only about one-tenth of those who departed the Russian capital returned to their homeland.

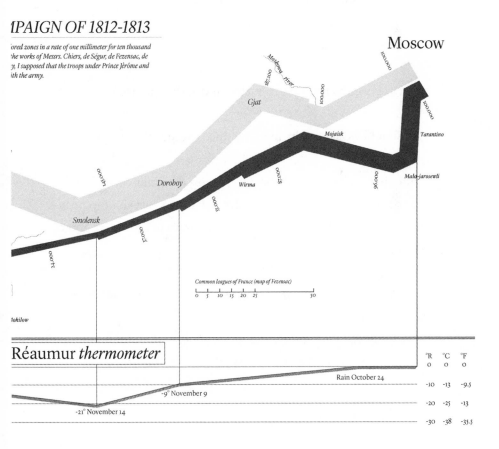

The journey started on June 24th and the soldiers didn't reach Moscow until mid-September. When the army was halfway to Moscow (the upper band in the middle of the chart), it had already lost most of the men who began the march. Yet the march continued, ultimately claiming the lives of another 100,000 soldiers.

A DAILY DILEMMA

Thankfully, we are many generations removed from nineteenth-century warfare, and most of us do not shoulder the burden of planning military campaigns. Yet every day we face decisions of go-or-stop, old-or-new, keep-at-it-or-change-direction. Sometimes these are high-impact, strategic choices, and many times they are more mundane:

- "Is it time to hire a new printing vendor?"

- "Do I need to tear up this memo and start again from scratch?"

- "Should we cancel the meeting since two people dropped out?"

These judgment calls are not clear-cut. Success demands commitment, and along the way there is resistance. It's not always easy to keep pushing ahead, which is probably why there is a library of life advice about persistence and staying on course:

"You can't change horses in mid-stream."
"Rome wasn't built in a day."
"When the going gets tough, the tough get going."
"You have to dance with the one you brought to the prom."

That last phrase is often seasoned with the twang and grammar of a Texas football coach: "You gotta dance with thum that brung ya." But with or without the accent, the proverbs are persuasive.

THE COST OF REFUSING TO CHANGE COURSE

Does this conventional wisdom actually help us, or is it toxic advice? The answer matters because the consequences of staying on the wrong track can be momentous. Even without the lives of thousands of soldiers in the balance, the choices we make affect our health, our relationships, our finances, and our reputations.

Resistance to changing course is so pervasive that its impact can be hard to measure. But if we reflect on our own lives, we can probably acknowledge times when we wish we had made a change sooner. We know people who spent too long pursuing the wrong career, the wrong goal, or the wrong relationship, even when it seemed clear to those around them that things would not end well.

On teams and in the workplace, the cost of taking the wrong course too far is just as familiar. Nearly every sales team has stories of pursuing a prospect for months at great cost before finally acknowledging they were not going to buy. Or we know of times when management seemed to blindly keep working with a troubled employee, hoping things would improve despite contrary evidence. Or episodes when a company just wouldn't pull the plug on a project even though it kept losing money.

We won't spend much time digging into the obvious costs of persisting in the wrong direction: wasted time, wasted money, and missed opportunities. In short, good money follows bad money.

Less obvious costs include loss of team effectiveness, damage to reputation or credibility, and discouragement. Prolonged stress related to negative circumstances or difficult relationships can lead to all sorts of health problems. It does not overstate the case to say that in staying on the wrong path too long can lead to sickness and sometimes death—even if you are not at war.

The words "it's too late" are like a prison sentence handed down from a judge as punishment for the crimes of the past. In fact, the meaning is very close to the primary definition of the word *damn*, according to the Merriam-Webster dictionary:

Damn: to condemn to a punishment or fate; *especially*: to condemn to hell.

While the word damn is used casually in today's language, its original meaning was an eternal curse. Isn't it also a type of curse to believe that it's too late to change something?

Every hour on the wrong path is time gone forever. Just one better decision for you and your team to correct your course can be worth the time spent reading this book—and it could save you thousands of dollars. It might even prevent a greater tragedy.

You Can "Change Horses"

Different strains of "it's too late" show up in our language in many ways. One version that endures—a full century into the age of the automobile—is the advice that "you can't change horses in mid-stream." Is that true? I'm not a horseman, but I would think it depends upon three factors:

- The horse

- The rider

- The stream

If my horse were struggling under my weight through rapids, wouldn't it be smart to at least try moving to a stronger steed (for the horse's sake and my own)?

It may be too late to avoid the negative consequences from past decisions and actions. But that doesn't mean you cannot shape the future in a radically different way. Indeed, sometimes we are far too pessimistic in judging what we can change today that will make tomorrow better.

In the business world, past actions sometimes would seem to pigeonhole a company in a particular market. In other cases, it seems too late to change customer perception or to challenge the acknowledged leader in the field. Consider some dramatic examples in which companies broke free from their historic product offering or market position:

- After selling equipment and hardware for half a century, it was too late for IBM to move to software and service. After all, their name was "International Business *Machines*." Their success in this reinvention is described in Lou Gerstner's aptly titled *Teaching Elephants to Dance*.

- In 1973 it was too late for Honda to challenge Harley-Davidson in selling motorcycles. Harley had 77 percent market share in the U.S. Yet just seven years later, Harley's share had decreased to 31 percent… far behind market-leader Honda.

- Following Honda's surge, it was too late for Harley-Davidson— nicknamed "Hardly Ableson" and "Hardly Driveable" in the late 1970s due to poor quality—to recover the reputation of their brand. Yet within twenty years, they were known again as the standard of quality and loyalty (and almost certainly owned the most tattooed brand in the world).

- It was too late for Samsung to successfully challenge Nokia on mobile phones. Yet in just five years, from 2007 to 2012, Nokia's market share plunged from over 50 percent at its peak to less than 4 percent, and in the same period Samsung's market share climbed to over 30 percent.

These illustrations reveal that large enterprises can in fact change course. Before the turnarounds, any analyst or journalist would have been forgiven for calling those strategies farfetched, unrealistic, and even wasteful.

LATE TO THE MOVIE

Was it too late for Blockbuster Video—the titan of bricks-and-mortar movie rental stores—to shift their model to movie-by-mail? Looking closely at their rival Netflix offers several examples—both positive and negative—of too-late thinking.

Netflix created and dominated the movie-by-mail category, and in the course of a few years wiped thousands of video-rental stores out of the strip malls. As bandwidth increased, Netflix offered streaming video as well as mailed DVDs. By mid-2011, Netflix had more subscriptions for its streaming video than for its original mail business and CEO Reed Hastings announced that Netflix would split into two companies. Netflix would offer only streaming video over the internet, and the DVD-by-mail business would now be transitioned to a separate company called Qwikster. Hastings explained:

> Most companies that are great at something… do not become great at new things people want because they are afraid to hurt their initial business. Eventually these companies realize their error of not focusing enough on the new thing, and then the company fights desperately and hopelessly to recover.

This justification rightly summarizes the importance of being able and willing to change. Yet the forward-looking move was met with disdain. Customers were angered by the notion of having to maintain two separate services and use two different websites. Investors protested as well, as the news of the split, combined with a planned price hike, caused Netflix stock to drop by 50 percent over a few months.

What Netflix did next was perhaps the most surprising piece of this story: they changed their plans. After months of work and planning, after creating a new brand and company, they put the split on hold. Instead, the company kept both the streaming and mailing arms of their business under the same brand and website (announced October 2011).

Surely there were some on the Netflix team who were committed to moving ahead with the plan to split into two companies. After all, it was a well-considered, forward-thinking business strategy and every bold move brings out the critics. Yet when we look at the success and tenfold stock rise of Netflix in the four years following the aborted company split, it's hard to escape the conclusion that they made the right choice by changing their plans.

WAS A DIFFERENT ENDING POSSIBLE?

It's encouraging to see a team that fought the notion of "it's too late" and ended up winning big. Keeping those turnarounds in mind, we can play "what-if" with some other famous businesses. Was it too late for Kodak to enter the market of digital cameras? Was it too late for Border's Books to shift operations online? We don't know the answers, but we can safely assume that somewhere in the leadership of those failed companies, someone was saying "it's too late to change our strategy now."

Is someone on your team saying the same thing?

CONFIRMATION BIAS

As we analyze the Expensive Sentence "It's too late to turn back now," it will help to understand why it takes root in the first place. Why are we inclined to continue on the wrong path instead of changing? More specifically, what would cause a person to drive too far the wrong way without stopping to get directions or check a map? Why would someone continue to date a person when everyone around them can see it's the wrong pick? How could smart generals march another hundred thousand men to their death after already losing as many?

Part of the answer is quite obvious: we don't like to be wrong. Even those of us who are humble, who love to learn, and who pride ourselves on being open-minded would far rather be right than wrong. This is more than a preference; it is a deep motivator that works at a subconscious level to filter the information we accept and shape how we interpret that information.

Imagine that you need a new car. After extensive online research and several test drives, you decide that it's time for a minivan and you pick the best model. You negotiate a price with the dealer, put down your money, and drive home in the shiny set of wheels.

What happens next—in almost all cases—is that your brain unconsciously seeks data and interprets it to confirm the decision you made. You hear of a smart friend who bought the same car. You find that it fits perfectly in your garage. You realize that it matches your favorite coat. You see that gas prices just went down, so you feel validated for buying a bigger vehicle.

This subconscious affirmation is called confirmation bias, and it plays out with virtually every decision we make. It's not just a coincidence or some form of wishful thinking; it is how human brains work. The phenomenon has been studied extensively by psychologists and neuroscientists. Confirmation bias helps explain why first impressions are so important and so lasting: after someone meets us and makes an initial judgment about what kind of person we are, that person's brain tends to find and accept data that correlates with that first impression.

There's nothing especially problematic about confirmation bias when you're choosing a restaurant for dinner or enjoying your new car. Your conclusions might not withstand a legal trial, but what does it matter? You might as well enjoy life rather than fret it away in endless analysis. In fact, our brains take these shortcuts out of necessity: there is so much incoming information that the brain actively tries to avoid revisiting a decision that it has already made.

Confirmation bias is obviously dangerous when it impairs our assessment of important decisions. When the stakes are high, we cannot afford to have prior decisions distort our perception of reality. We must see the world as it is, and not simply as we wish to see it.

The American wars in Vietnam and Iraq are widely seen as campaigns in which confirmation bias resulted in the loss of many lives. While those conflicts may be accessible examples of confirmation bias at a strategic level—that is, the question of whether to begin or continue military action—it is safe to assume that every war has produced casualties due to confirmation bias at a tactical level. Just as Napoleon and his generals continued their march at the cost of many lives, untold military leaders have been slow to see a better course because they were unconsciously and illogically justifying the decisions they had already made.

The principle holds true in medicine, where lives are lost because caretakers or patients chose to follow the wrong course of treatment too long. These mistakes are also prevalent when human lives are not at stake. Dollars and entire companies have been lost when managers failed to consider information that contradicted their beliefs.

We cannot eliminate confirmation bias, but we can defang it. As with any bias, confirmation bias is much less dangerous when it is openly acknowledged and evaluated. At a personal or group level, it is helpful to ask whether beliefs are formed as a result of data or whether data is considered because of beliefs. Beliefs and information can have a chicken-and-egg relationship; in which it is not always clear which came first.

Finding the Line between Perseverance and Stubbornness

Every Expensive Sentence must be considered in context. The circumstances surrounding the sentiment to "stay the course" can shed light on whether that advice is affirming the right path or enabling the wrong path. Let's consider when the sentence is helpful.

Perseverance is a time-honored virtue, endorsed by sages from the classic times ("He conquers who endures"—Persius) through the industrial age ("Genius is 1% inspiration and 99% perspiration"—Thomas Edison). In today's short-attention-span, commitment-averse culture, it can seem like the quality of persistence is in short supply. Maybe we'd all be better off with some good old-fashioned "stick-to-it-ive-ness."

Indeed, when sloth or doubt threaten, it's helpful to hear some encouragement to keep at it. We need to be reminded of our decisions and commitments, affirm why we made them in the first place, and press on through difficulty.

The encouragement to persevere is most helpful in specific circumstances:

- **COLD FEET** — When we voice doubts in the early stages of action, before we've earnestly begun something that we thoughtfully decided to do or before we have had any chance to gauge the results.
- **HOT HEAD** — When we're feeling tired or frustrated in the moment and are vulnerable to making an emotional decision that we might regret after a good night's sleep or with more perspective.
- **ALMOST THERE** — When we are very close to the finish line and may lose sight of the fact that just a small amount of added effort will secure a worthwhile milestone.
- **DUTY CALLS** — When we have a moral or legal commitment to a course of action, or for other reasons have no reasonable options.

By no means are these the only cases in which the best decision would ultimately be to forge ahead. But if you can't quickly peg the situation as one of those listed above, it probably warrants more thorough reflection before plowing onward.

So "keep at it" is great advice... some of the time. Persistence is necessary, but persistence must be informed by reality. When persistence becomes blind stubbornness, it can keep us on the wrong path and do terrible harm.

The obstinate flavor of "it's too late to change" is commonplace and usually self-administered. In the workplace it might sound like this:

"After all we've put into this implementation, we can't put the brakes on now."

"We've been investing in the project for three years… we're not going to walk away!"

"Andre's been here forever. We can't let him go now."

"I've been negotiating this deal for months and I'm not about to let it fall through."

Are these statements of admirable persistence or bald stubbornness? Or could it be a mix of both: admirable stubbornness? We can usually find the root by answering a few questions.

Question 1: Are Your Eyes Open or Closed?

There may be moments when it's helpful to ignore the fluster around us and finish a task. But focus and persistence don't grant us permission to be ignorant. This quote from Henry Ward Beecher goes directly to the motivation:

> *The difference between perseverance and obstinacy is that one comes from a strong will, and the other from a strong won't.*

If someone isn't even willing to entertain the notion of change, her stance is more likely related to stubbornness or fear than borne of noble persistence. It's natural to resist data that challenges our course, but diligence cannot overcome denial. Avoiding distractions is not the same as willfully ignoring reality.

For two years I led a chapter of a national forum for CEOs. The group had a favorite motto that we often repeated: "Reality is always your friend." It was a helpful reminder because even the highly successful leaders we worked with often resisted hearing what they didn't want to hear. But we could all acknowledge—if we stopped to think it through—that while negative feedback can be tough to hear and costly to accept, it is necessary for growth and success. Instead of rejecting contrary information, we're better off listening and considering whether it might be time to change course.

Question 2: Are You Looking Forward or Looking Backward?

The objections to change discussed above have a common characteristic: they all reference history. The cited reasons for keeping on course are things that were done or decided in the past.

Yesterday's actions shouldn't drive today's decisions. When reasons spring from the past, it likely means that sentimentality and emotion are trumping data and reason. Sometimes one simple question can cut through this Expensive Sentence: is this decision about what's best for the future or about what happened in the past?

Question 3: Which Is the Easier Path?

Often we resist the changes that are costly in the near term, without fully valuing how they will make life easier down the road. Imagine that you walk into a supermarket and take an empty grocery cart. Once that cart is moving, it requires very little energy to keep it headed straight forward. To stop the cart quickly or turn its direction takes more physical exertion than to let it keep rolling.

Now imagine that you've been shopping for half an hour, and the cart is full of cans, bottles, meats, cheeses, and produce. (No bread or chips—we don't need the carbs and they don't help the illustration.) When it's rolling, the cart still doesn't require much of a push to keep it headed straight, but turning now requires more strength than it did before.

This momentum principle applies to our activities: it's usually much easier in the short term to keep going in the same direction. The longer we have been on the path and the more people that are involved, the harder it is to change. Since changing course takes more work, perseverance can be a cover for laziness.

As you are evaluating a potential change in course, ask the question: "Which would be more work in the near term: keeping at it or making a change?" The answer is not conclusive by itself: just because one path requires more immediate effort, that doesn't necessarily make it the best choice. But if more effort is required to change, it's more likely that resistance or plain laziness could underlie the desire to stay on course.

CHECKING OUR RATIONALE

Let's recap the three self-diagnosis questions:

1. Are we open to new information or closed?

2. Are we basing this decision on the future, or are we clouded by the past?

3. Would it be easier to change or easier to stay on course?

We need to examine ourselves candidly and often because momentum and conventional wisdom can tell us it's too late to change. That may be exactly what we want to hear. Just as we hate to throw out the too-tight jeans that remind us of a leaner past, sometimes our team holds on to a plan that was made when reality looked different—and more to our liking. Nostalgia or sentimentality sometimes encourage us to stick with our poor decisions instead of improving them.

UNDERSTANDING SWITCHING COSTS

After we recognize that we can make a change, we are free to look at the data and evaluate our options. That analysis requires an accurate understanding of two key economic terms:

- Switching costs

- Sunk costs

These concepts are familiar to all of us, but are widely misunderstood in practice.

SWITCHING COSTS

Switching costs are the one-time costs associated with a transition from one operational setup to another. For example, to change from cable TV to satellite TV, you may have to buy a satellite receiver and pay an installation fee. Switching costs also include time. If you switch from your old accountant to a new accountant, you probably will need to spend time explaining your finances and history.

Switching costs factor into all buying decisions because any pur-chase will mean a new product, a new vendor, a new technology, a new process, or all of the above. In my procurement experience, I have witnessed firsthand how hundreds of people evaluate switching costs.

In almost every case, our natural instincts seem to take us in one of two opposite directions, so that:

- Switching costs are greatly underestimated—that is, someone assumes that the change will be painless, quick, and cheap, or:

- Switching costs are greatly overestimated—someone believes that the change will be absolutely horrendous, with untold costs, headaches, and risks.

When there is resistance to change, it's more likely that the costs will be overestimated. Sometimes those costs skyrocket in the imagination.

ONE MILLION DOLLARS

Years ago I encouraged a *Fortune* 100 firm to evaluate their payroll provider. My suspicion was that the company could save several hundred thousand dollars by switching to a competitive vendor. I knew there would be resistance, and rightly so: when payroll is working smoothly, making a change is a huge risk. (One bad payroll run can lead to many unhappy people.) But beyond the risk, several people at the company gave me a specific financial objection: "The last time we switched, it cost us a million dollars to implement our payroll system."

Implementation always carries some cost, but to me this number seemed an order of magnitude too high. As I asked around the company, several people validated this million-dollar figure, but no one had specifics. I finally tracked down an IT director who had been on the team at the time of the previous change. To my great surprise, he too supported the million-dollar cost to change payroll companies. I asked him why it cost so much.

"Well, we had to migrate all of the employment data, bring together the different groups, install the timecard system, train all of the HR team."

I was puzzled. "All of that was necessary just to change the payroll provider?"

"Well, most of it was for the enterprise resource planning and accounting software we were switching out. But part of that was the payroll."

"Oh, so at the same time you were installing payroll, you were also changing the ERP and accounting software?"

"Yes. It was a brutal year."

"Well, if we wanted to change *just* the payroll provider… what would be involved?"

"That would be a much smaller job. No big deal."

After we got specific, it turned out that the only requirements would be two new interfaces. Given the time required for IT staff to build and test the interfaces thoroughly, we estimated the cost to be less than $40,000.

GETTING SPECIFIC TO GET REAL

The million-dollar implementation had become part of company lore. Teams are collections of people, and people have collectively bad memories. When your team begins to complain about its being "too late" to do anything because of the switching cost, it is important to challenge assumptions and direct the conversation to actual data:

"When we say it's too late, I guess we're talking about the investment we've put in so far. But obviously we *could* change if we needed to, right?

"What would it mean for us to change now? Have we scoped that out?"

"I agree that switching now sounds like a huge hassle, but let's talk about what the benefits would be."

As with all Expensive Sentences, "it's too late" is most powerful when left vague and general. When we bring in specifics and start to itemize the expenses, the costs often shrink. A simple qualifying phrase can be enormously helpful in pointing to the specific areas of cost:

"It's too late to change the product *without reprinting the marketing brochures.*"

"If we back out of the contract now, *we will lose our earnest money.*"

"The invitations have gone out, *so changing the date would be a big hassle.*"

Any of those sentences are far better than the declarative "It's too late" because at least they preserve options. The door may be hard to open, but it's not closed and locked.

A related snare is to fold into switching costs expenses that would be incurred even without a change. The classic example of that is the person claiming it's too late to switch careers because "If I start school now, I'll be 50 before I'm finished in six years." The important follow-up question is: how old will you be in six years if you don't start now?

It's too late to change the past, but it's the perfect time to make sure we're not trapped in it. Speaking of the past, let's turn to the second and more sinister problem with this Expensive Sentence.

AVOIDING THE QUICKSAND OF SUNK COSTS

A realistic view of switching costs can demystify change and make decisions more fact-based. But you might not even get to that part of the decision if you don't escape the greedy quicksand of sunk costs.

Resources that have been used and cannot be recovered are what economists call *sunk costs*. "Sunk cost" is an elegantly simple label for a concept that we all understand: what has been done cannot be undone, and what's gone is gone.

In economics and financial projections, there is an equally simple way to treat sunk costs: you ignore them. If we're scoping out our building maintenance costs for next year, it doesn't matter that two years ago we invested in a major landscaping project. If you're planning the food budget for May, the big holiday parties the prior December don't come into play. They are history.

Those examples sound simple enough, but in practice it's easy to entangle past and future costs together. Moreover, sunk costs apply to time and effort as well as to money.

DRIVING THE WRONG WAY

Imagine that you and an old school friend are driving to a classmate's wedding at a winery. It's in a rural area that you're not familiar with, your phones don't have reception, and your GPS does not seem to be working. Trying to remember the directions someone told you, you have exited the interstate, made two turns just as described, and are now on the smaller country road where you believe the winery is located.

You have a feeling that you have driven past the winery, but you keep driving on. Now suddenly your GPS perks up and figures out where you are. It turns out that the winery is about ten minutes away—in the opposite direction.

You swear out of frustration and pull the car over to turn around.

Then your friend pipes in: "Gosh, we've already spent about twenty minutes going in this direction; let's keep going and we'll find another road to take us to the winery."

You pause for a minute and then laugh because obviously your friend is joking. The time you spent driving the wrong way is completely irrelevant at this time. Only two things matter now: the location of the winery and your location.

Do We Really Believe That Sunk Costs Are Gone?

The context of driving reveals how absurd it is to let sunk costs—specifically, the mistake of driving in the wrong direction—influence decisions. You may be struggling to think of a friend so irrational that he or she would argue to keep driving. (Or then again, maybe someone leaps to mind.)

But despite logic, sunk costs often play a dominant role in the decisions we make. Like the friend who somehow can't admit defeat in driving the wrong direction, we often hold past decisions and actions at the front of our minds even though we can't change them.

The fact is that humans are terrible at ignoring sunk costs. Economists and psychologists have proven this with numerous studies. As an example, here is a question posed to sixty-one subjects in a 1985 study by Hal Arkes and Catherine Blumer at Ohio University. Read it carefully, as if you were being asked to respond:

Assume that you have spent $100 on a ticket for a weekend ski trip to Michigan. Several weeks later you buy a $50 ticket for a weekend ski trip to Wisconsin. You think you will enjoy the Wisconsin ski trip more than the Michigan ski trip. As you are putting your just-purchased Wisconsin ski trip ticket in your wallet, you notice that the Michigan ski trip and the Wisconsin ski trip are for the same weekend! It's too late to sell either ticket, and you cannot return either one. You must use one ticket and not the other. As honestly as you can, answer to yourself: which trip would you go on?

The results of the study were informative: more than half of the respondents—33 out of 61—chose the more expensive Michigan ski trip, even with the stipulated assumption that they would enjoy it less than the $50 trip to Wisconsin.[2]

If you were in the minority that made the future-based decision, then congratulations are in order. But consider the variants of sunk-cost thinking we hear every day:

- "I'd just spent $1500 fixing the engine, so I figured I should keep the car."

- "We'd spent two months planning for that meeting; I wasn't about to cancel."

- "The invitations went out already and family members bought their plane tickets, so we weren't going to postpone the wedding."

The irrelevance of the time driving in the wrong direction is no different from the sunk costs in these examples. The past investment should have no bearing on the future. The same goes in the workplace, though we may hear many Expensive Sentences on our teams:

- "We've been with this PR agency for two years."

29

- "We've already put $250K into this advertising campaign."

- "The sales guy's numbers are still poor, but he's been here two years and I hate to let him go."

As thorny as these objections may be, they are not the hardest. It's tougher still when your friend says about her boyfriend, "Yeah, Hank has some issues, but we've been together for four years. I'd hate to throw all of that away." This is not a book about relationships, but I mention this example because most of us know someone who dated the wrong person too long, and some of us *were* the person who dated the wrong person too long. Those costs are not trivial.

Am I saying that you definitely should fire that PR agency, buy a new car, and that your friend should dump her boyfriend? Not necessarily; each of those decisions deserves care and thought. The point is that the evaluation must be based on the future, not on the past. The amount of money spent, the good times together, the effort put into training someone recently—those are all sunk costs. If you are trying to make the best decision, past investments are irrelevant.

DON'T JUST IGNORE SUNK COSTS—ACTIVELY REJECT THEM

Part of the danger of sunk costs is that we don't recognize their power. The language we use in reference to sunk costs is not strong enough, in my opinion. Economists say we are to ignore sunk costs—which is fitting instruction in a clinical decision process or when we're making a cost model. But in real life, too often we ignore sunk costs in a different way: we don't recognize their impact on our thinking, so they seep into our decision-making.

Ignoring sunk costs isn't working. We have to see them and actively reject them. In the context of making decisions:

- The present matters—what you have and what you know.

- The future matters—where you are going.

- The past does NOT matter—that is, the decisions and investments from yesterday should not drive the choices of today.

The right decision today requires a clear-eyed assessment of the best information at hand, without a wistful desire to hold onto yesterday's choices.

Kill Your Darlings

Good writers know the danger of sunk costs. After you've spent three hours writing a front-page article, or three months writing a book, it can be difficult to accept editing that reveals major flaws. A writer who has sweat, time, and passion invested in a piece would much rather hear that only minor tweaks are needed than face a complete rewrite.

Creative works are birthed and may feel like the flesh and blood of the creator. From that sentiment comes the advice that you must be able to "kill your darlings." If any artist wants to create great work, she must be able to look at her own creations that fail to meet that standard, crumple them up, and toss them aside.

We are all artists creating our lives and our futures. Letting the past shape our future is like holding onto mediocre old drafts. Yes, those drafts took time to create, but we know we can do much better.

Nor should mistakes or poor choices condemn us. The book of Psalms describes forgiveness as the ultimate freedom from the past:

He has removed our sins as far from us as the east is from the west.[3]

This language is poetic and profound. Wherever you are on the map, "the east" is as far as you can imagine in one direction, and "the west" is all the way out in the exact opposite direction.

When you are planning, keep your sunk costs as far from your plans as the east is from the west. Whether your sunk costs are business mistakes, bad drafts, or poor personal choices, take bold measures to ensure that your decisions about the future are not contaminated by decisions from the past.

WISE REPLIES TO "IT'S TOO LATE TO TURN BACK NOW"

. . . .

We have reviewed the costs and the concepts, and now it's time to get practical. In the remainder of this chapter we will review sample language, conversation topics, and exercises that you can apply with your team to avoid getting stuck.

RESPONDING DIRECTLY TO EXPENSIVE SENTENCES

The best time to contain the cost of an Expensive Sentence is just after it is said. The next time you hear "it's too late to turn back," or "I've put way too much time and effort into [x] to change now," try a reply along these lines:

> *Tommy, you are not one to throw in the towel when things get a bit rough or take longer than we'd hoped. I love that, and I'm with you. I guess I'm wondering if knowing everything we know now we would still hire Green & Associates for this project."*

> *I don't buy into the idea that it's too late to change. Sure, the best time to plant a tree is twenty years ago. But the second best time is today. Let's make the right decisions for the future."*

> *It seems like we've gone pretty far in that direction, and I know it may seem like giving up or admitting failure to change course now. But it's OK to learn and to make mistakes. Let's stop saying 'we did this' or 'we spent that' and focus on what we have and what we know."*

> **❝** *Changing might be a big job, but maybe we're overestimating the effort and cost. Can we spend ten minutes talking through the details of what it would take to change course? Maybe that will clarify whether it's a good idea, or confirm that it really is better to keep going as we are."*

GROUP CONVERSATION TOPICS

Reducing confirmation bias to make better decisions is a worthy pursuit. To achieve that end, consider the three principles listed below. Read the sections and then ask the discussion questions on your team.

Decisions Are Different from Results

Good decisions can lead to bad results. This seems clear enough in writing, but in practice the distinction between decisions and results can get muddy. Changing plans does not necessarily mean that the prior approach was faulty or that the original decision was wrong. Circumstances change, and information improves with the course of time.

Basketball coaches understand that just because a player's shot doesn't go in the basket, it wasn't necessarily a bad shot to take. Throughout sports, success is largely driven by playing the percentages: choosing the scenario that is most likely to lead to success. Even so, the right decision can often lead to the less-preferred outcome. That is part of the game.

It's also true that bad decisions can produce good outcomes. This occurrence introduces the danger of false confidence: you might think you were smart when you were just lucky. But if we embrace the distinction between decisions and outcomes, we allow the possibility that a good outcome doesn't always imply the right process. We also are liberated to know that making a new decision based on better information does not mean that a prior decision was wrong.

Discussion Questions:

- Do we know the difference between decisions and results?

- Can we identify times recently when good decisions led to bad results, or times when poor decisions had good outcomes?

WE SHOULD EXPECT (AND BUDGET FOR) SOME POOR DECISIONS

It's okay to be wrong. We all make mistakes and bad decisions sometimes. When there is freedom to fail and room to correct our errors, we can experiment, adjust, learn, and improve. If we expect these iterations and acknowledge that failure is part of the process, we are less likely to accept the false premise that it's too late to change.

Pause for a moment and consider the culture on your team and in your family. Do those around you feel free to fail? When they have to correct course, are they extended grace and given encouragement, or are they subtly—or perhaps not so subtly—scolded and frowned upon? Now consider your own attitudes about being right and making mistakes. When you have to admit to yourself that you were wrong, are you upset with yourself or can you laugh it off?

Discussion Questions:

- Is it more important on our team to be right or to be effective?

- How have we demonstrated that we can make mistakes and move forward?

35

MEASURED REFLECTION IS HEALTHY

My Dad loved to say, "He who hesitates is lost." Though I have a warm spot for that expression, it probably should be administered with a parallel warning: he who doesn't hesitate may sometimes become more lost. The balance between action and reflection can fail in either direction, from analysis-paralysis on one side to reckless motion without a plan on the other side. When a team goes from one bold course directly to another, leaving wreckage in its wake, it may indicate a culture in which thoughtful reflection needs more emphasis.

Discussion Questions:

- Do we have a good balance between action and reflection?

- When have we erred on the side of acting too quickly, and how did that work out?

- Where are we being too reflective and not acting quickly enough?

We can apply these principles to the Netflix example. Clearly Netflix had a culture that embraced change and valued reflection—otherwise they would not have introduced the bold move to split the companies. From their response to the market and press reactions, Netflix demonstrated that their culture also was open to admitting it was wrong and recognized the difference between a decision and results.

EXERCISES TO AVOID SUNK COSTS AND ASSESS SWITCHING COSTS

. . . .

The following tactics can move your decisions from assumptions and generalities to facts and sound reasoning.

EXERCISE: "WE KNOW [X]. WE HAVE [Y]."

Remember that simply trying to ignore sunk costs does not work. Acknowledge that sunk costs are likely to be present in your team's thinking, and take active measures to reject them. This exercise in disciplined language is simple and powerful.

History versus Assets

One of the reasons sunk costs have such power is the sense that there must be some value of decisions and actions from the past. Indeed, there is value, but it's important to be precise with our language. It's not what we did that matters from the past: it is what we now have and what we now know. Consider these examples:

- If you just spent $2500 on a new transmission for your car, then the car has a new transmission. In theory, that should last for years without requiring any investment. There is value in that new transmission (though it may be less than the $2500 paid).

- If you have a teammate who has been with you for two years, you may have developed deep trust in that person. That person may have specific knowledge about your company and industry that will help him be more effective in his job. There is value in the trust and the knowledge; those are assets.

- It is irrelevant that you have spent $75,000 on development of a new system to improve customer service. What is relevant (or at least may be) is the asset that you have: a nearly finished system.

Assets may exist because of the time and money spent, but their value in the future is independent from the past investment.

Using the Right Language

To ensure that the past does not pollute team decisions, you can enforce the use of precise language that will keep discussions future-focused. When you hear "we've already spent X amount of time or X amount of dollars," convert that language into the only things that matter:

- We know _____.

- We have _____.

This exercise requires practice and discipline, especially in situations when the value of the assets don't measure up to the money and time we spent acquiring them. Rejecting sunk costs requires both knowledge and resolve.

EXERCISE: MODEL FUTURE COSTS

The right view of the future compares the costs and benefits of different scenarios that correspond to the choices at hand. A cost model is an organized way to compare those scenarios. In its simplest form, a cost model is little more than a list of the different categories of costs.

Imagine that you were considering an office move to a nearby building that would be lower rent. A co-worker objects, "it's too late to move; we've set up all of our equipment here." To address that potentially Expensive Sentence in a cost model, you would assess the costs for staying and moving over a period of time—maybe three years would be reasonable for an office move.

	STAY	MOVE
YEAR ONE		
Mover Cost	$0	$2,000
Equipment Setup	$0	$2,000
Rent	$14,000	$11,000
YEAR TWO		
Rent	$14,000	$11,000
YEAR THREE		
Rent	$14,000	$11,000
TOTAL COSTS	*$42,000*	*$37,000*

Cost models for big projects can get highly complex, and any model that projects new sales or other unknowns will rely on assumptions. But for evaluating change, a simple cost model will often reveal the truth and move a conversation from the imaginary to the factual. (There are several cost model examples and templates at the website *ExpensiveSentences.com*.)

EXERCISE: TAKE ON A "TOO LATE"

We've considered some dramatic victories where companies did not accept that it was too late to change, and we've seen stories where too-late thinking may have condemned teams to poor outcomes.

The future is unwritten, at work and at home. Can you identify any areas where you may be vulnerable to believing that it's too late to change? Some of the questions below may spark your thinking.

- Is it too late for your company to change product lines to be more competitive?

- Is it too late for your family to finally get the house organized or develop better communication?

- Is it too late for your church to serve a different group of people?

- It is too late to improve a relationship with your sibling, parent, or child?

- Is it too late for you to learn a new language or a new musical instrument?

- Is it too late to change your diet, start exercising, or take on other healthy habits?

These questions may stir pangs of regret or sadness. You may feel the sting of wishing you had changed years ago. But it is important to cast off those feelings and look ahead. It is NOT too late to change. As the ancient proverb states:

"The best time to plant a tree is twenty years ago. The second best time to plant a tree is today."

CHAPTER 2

"WE'RE TOO SWAMPED TO DEAL WITH THAT NOW"

*"That sounds like a good idea, but I'm up to
my neck in alligators."*

*"I haven't been able to start exercising yet;
maybe when things calm down."*

*"It's been so crazy recently I haven't been able
to get to that."*

*"We'll have to consider that after we get out of
survival mode."*

Let me take a moment to thank you for reading this book.

I commend you, because unless your boss is giving you a test on *Expensive Sentences* tomorrow, reading this book is not an urgent matter for you. Other worthy pursuits could be keeping you busy right now, and yet you choose to read this book.

Sadly, far more people will buy this book and never read it than will get to this page in the text. That's true for most books (even those that might be better than this one). Why do people leave excellent books unread after they pay good money for them? Often it's because they intend to read the books, but they "just don't have the time." They are swamped.

I empathize with super-busy people because I've been swamped myself. I've been busy with important things, and at times I've been busy with decidedly unimportant things. Being busy is not bad in itself. But busyness can be extremely costly, both in business and in your personal life.

You've probably seen firsthand how being "too busy" can lead to wasted money and time:

- Too busy to change your phone plan, so you overpay $30 each month for months

- Too busy to maintain the car, leading to a costly repair

- Too busy seeking new customers to visit an old customer... who leaves

- Too busy on tactics to revisit a strategy, which turns out to be deeply flawed

- Too busy to get to the gym and exercise, so you don't sleep as well and have less energy

- Too busy to hire someone to help you be less busy

- Too busy to train someone you have already hired to take work off of your plate

Do any of these sound familiar? Not every instance of being busy will carry a high cost. But when leaders believe they are too busy to make a good decision or take the right action, then "we're swamped" becomes an Expensive Sentence. The costs that follow include missed opportunities and lost money. Ironically, too much busyness often leads to wasted time—and then more reason to be busy.

Is "We're too swamped to look at that now" an Expensive Sentence for you or your team? Let's explore a few of the ways that busyness can cost money—and often much more.

Too Busy to Save Money

For years I have helped companies review expenses, negotiate with vendors, and find savings. Often I'll connect with a business leader after speaking at an event or introducing myself at a networking meeting. A CEO will approach me and say something along the lines of "Jack, we really could use your help. I know we're spending too much."

Then I'll ask some questions and share my approach, and we'll trade business cards. What happens next—in most cases—is nothing.

Of course I'll follow up, but typically months go by before the next step, if that even happens at all. Sometimes we'll reconnect months later, and the CEO will say, "Jack, I still want to get you in here. We've just been swamped."

This doesn't hurt my feelings (any more) because I know that a company leader has a full plate. But are these companies really working on more important matters?

Success in business is ultimately defined by two numbers: the amount coming in (revenue) and the amount going out (costs). The math is simple. Sadly, even though the importance of controlling costs is universally recognized, many companies suffer losses, layoffs, and bankruptcy because they can't keep their expenses under control.

IMPORTANT BUT NOT URGENT

The challenge I face in my work is the lack of urgency. It's almost never urgent for a company to reduce expenses by three or four percent, any more than it is urgent for someone to eat more vegetables to improve his health. But when health fails, it's not feasible to go back and change what you've eaten for the last three years. In a similar way, when saving money becomes urgent, it's sometimes beyond the time when small changes can make a big difference. Saving even ten or twenty percent may not be enough, and the busyness that kept the leaders from addressing costs now threatens their enterprise.

When we are too busy, we are often tending to urgent matters. These may or may not be important matters. Steven Covey addresses this subject with an important-vs.-urgent matrix in the book *First Things First*. Covey argues that the most effective leaders call attention to the important matters even when they are not urgent. In the short term, this means that some urgent (but not important) items must be delayed. In the longer term, it means there are fewer urgent matters to deal with because some of them are taken care of before they become urgent. But if only urgent matters are addressed, it is likely that more items will drift from important to urgent because of neglect. This self-fueling cycle is called the "tyranny of the urgent."[4]

"WHY DIDN'T WE DO THAT MONTHS AGO!"

Fortunately, I often get to help companies before their financial situation is urgent. On coaching projects, I work with the CFO and the purchasing team, reviewing expenses to find savings opportunities. We specify next steps for a number of items, and some of these steps are quite simple. For example:

- Make sure we are paying the contract rate on a specific purchase

- Ask the vendor to deliver only once a month instead of weekly

- Ask vendor A to quote a price on the product we're currently buying from vendor B

- Get three groups at the company to consolidate orders for better high-quantity pricing

These actions may require only a few emails or phone calls. When we follow up the next month, it's not unusual to report five-figure savings from just a few hours of work. Found money is always welcome, but team leaders have a bittersweet reaction as they look back and realize that they could have saved even more money with little effort. They ask themselves, "Why didn't we do that MONTHS ago?"

Maybe they didn't do it before because they didn't really believe it would help. Indeed, there's no guarantee that a given project will return big savings. I challenge my clients to identify five projects, and I forecast that they will see meaningful results on at least three of them (I've never had anyone tell me that my prediction hasn't held true).

We know one thing: if we don't even try something because we are too busy, we certainly will have no results. As Wayne Gretzky noted up in profoundly obvious wisdom: "you miss 100 percent of the shots you don't take."

TOO BUSY TO SAVE TIME

As essential as money is, time is arguably a more valuable resource. While you can make money—and sometimes even find money—I've never known anyone to make or find time (despite the popular expressions "I'll make the time..." or "I'll find the time..."). Given the finite quality of time, there are moments when spending time to save money may not be the right tradeoff.

But what if a time investment can save you *time?* The too-busy complaint can turn into a death spiral if being too busy makes you even more busy because you miss a chance to actually save time.

The business expression "it takes money to make money" explains that a financial investment may be necessary before a payout can be received. In a parallel principle, it's often true that it *takes time to make time.* Most paths to efficiency and time savings require an investment up front. Those who are too busy to make that investment will never enjoy the benefits.

As you consider your life and your team, are you dealing with important items before they become pressing problems? Are you taking steps to free time and avoid the tyranny of the urgent?

FIXING THE EZ PASS

Do you remember tossing quarters into toll baskets on interstates? This was a fun sport from the backseat of the family station wagon, but grew to be a nuisance as I hit driving age and journeyed through the Northeastern U.S. If you've never had that experience of carefully saving your quarters for weeks before a road trip, then counting out the right change and making sure it didn't drop on the ground, it's probably because you are young enough to enjoy the full benefit of the automated toll transponder—in my area called the "EZ Pass." (Or maybe you're blessed to live in an area without toll roads, and you've never known either.)

I got my first EZ Pass–type device in the mid-1990s, and the benefits were instant: less time in tollbooth lines, and no need to hunt for loose change. The EZ Pass is a sterling example of technology well deployed. It's easier for customers, it's less expensive for those who own the roads, and it eliminates one of the most monotonous jobs imaginable.

One day earlier this year—without any warning—the EZ Pass in our minivan fell off the windshield with a thud. It had been affixed with Velcro tape, and after a few years the adhesive on the tape apparently wore out. So it needed to be re-attached to the windshield. This was one of the rare automotive tasks I can actually handle myself, and yet weeks went by and the EZ Pass remained in the car door pocket.

Why did I procrastinate on this simple fix? First, I didn't have the Velcro tape handy, and it seemed like an effort to track that down at the store and make the time to fix it. Second, I felt like we didn't use the EZ Pass that often, and it really wasn't too much of a hassle to reach down and find the pass and hold it up when we needed it. Honestly, there was never a good time, and I was "too busy" to prioritize the fix.

So three months went by. Every time we hit a tollbooth, there were more costs than I cared to admit:

- Cost of stress: "Where's the EZ Pass? Am I holding it in the right place so the machine can read it?"

- Cost of regret: "Darn, I can't believe I didn't fix that yet. I have to do that next week."

- Cost of revisiting: "Where do I buy that Velcro tape? When am I going to be near that store?"

Finally—just a few short weeks before I wrote these words—I was at the store and noticed the Velcro tape. I bought it, and later that day spent two minutes re-attaching the EZ Pass. Wow, did I wish I had made that fix months earlier.

I share my EZ Pass misadventure because these little things have more cost than we realize, and fixing them often carries far more benefit than we appreciate. You can probably relate to this story in your life; my guess is that there are a few minor projects awaiting you at home that would improve your life in a small but noticeable way.

Tackle one tonight. You owe it to yourself and those around you to make the most of your time. Being "too busy" is about far more than productivity.

Too Busy to Save Relationships

As a child of the 1970s, I have strong memories of the Harry Chapin ballad *Cat's in the Cradle*. If you know that song, the title alone may stir up feelings of nostalgia or sadness. More than a textbook example of seventies melancholy, the song is a poignant tale about relationships and regret. The lyrics tell of a preoccupied father who was away on business trips and in the office late as his son went through the milestones of childhood. The dad was just too busy. Finally, after the father retired, he yearned to spend more time getting to know his now-adult son. But sadly, the son had grown up to be just like his dad—and was now too busy with his own life to spend time together.

Chapin admitted that the song had relevance to his own experience as a parent: "Frankly, this song scares me to death."[5] All of us have seen relationships suffer from lack of attention. In the personal sphere this can be tragic. The deathbed regret of "I should have spent more time with my family" may sound trite, but that doesn't lessen its pain for many who wish they had put more priority on relationships with loved ones.

If this topic speaks to you, you may want to take action right now. Feel free to put down the book to make a phone call or write a note. If nothing else, I hope you'll pause when you catch yourself saying you're too busy to connect with a friend or family member.

In the workplace, too, we know that ultimately nothing is more important than relationships. Money, strategy, products, and processes are all integral to business. But if these pursuits crowd out customer and employee relationships, a business cannot prosper for long.

When relationships falter, everything else becomes a rounding error. This is plainly true with our close friends and family, and work-based relationships can also suffer from a lack of time and tending.

Customers

In the 1980s, marketers and financial analysts began paying explicit attention to the "lifetime value" of customers. This focus brought more attention to the fact that it is almost always less expensive to keep an existing customer than to acquire a new one. Yet decades later, many sales organizations are far more focused on getting new customers than on maintaining current ones. When chasing a huge new contract or the next "whale" customer makes your team too busy to maintain current relationships, the risk of losing your old customers grows.

EMPLOYEES

Engaged employees are more productive. To be fully engaged, employees must connect to the mission and must believe that company leadership values them. One of the most effective ways to demonstrate that employees are valued is to communicate with care and consistency.

I worked at a company where the CEO announced that he wanted to adopt numerous new benefits for the employees, including more training, company picnics, and incentive programs. Three years later none of this was in place. Some of the employees concluded that management was too busy to take care of things that mattered to them, and indeed some left the company.

PURSUING BAD NEWS

In relationships, things don't go wrong all at once. When small cracks appear in relationships—personal or professional—busyness can combine with denial to create a dangerous dynamic of avoidance. The worst time to be too busy is when many of us would prefer to be: when bad news surfaces.

Again I'll offer the proviso that this is not a book on customer relationships, employee relationships, or family relationships *per se,* but our examination of the costs of busyness would be incomplete without including how we relate to those around us. When we are busy to the point of harming important relationships, it's worth examining our schedule and priorities.

Which one of these statements best describes you:

- You are busy building your most important relationships.

- Your busyness is damaging your most important relationships.

There's a saying attributed to an old country preacher: "If the devil can't make you bad, he'll make you busy!" The surprising warning reveals the seductive danger of busyness, and the power of the Expensive Sentence "I'm just too swamped to do that now." Busyness usually appears in the form of something good, but it can distract us from what is better.

Too Busy to Decide: The Cost of Revisiting

My mother would often remind me that "not to decide is to decide." That's an insightful truth about many of life's activities. If we postpone a decision about joining a group, taking a class, or starting a hobby, those opportunities are often overcome by events. Then, as John Lennon observed, "Life is what happens to you while you're busy making other plans."

But sometimes too much of life *becomes* making plans when a poorly contained decision-making process oozes into days and weeks. In those cases, the cost of indecision extends beyond the missed opportunity. The shot-we-don't-take or decision-we-don't-make lingers unresolved, sucking up more time and mental energy every time we revisit it.

Decisions Are Like Accordions

My wife picked out our wedding cake in fifteen minutes. We happened upon a nice-looking bakery between appointments, strolled in, and got it done. There were no subsequent discussions about "gosh, maybe we should get the strawberry filling" or "is four tiers too much?" It was a short engagement, so we had to plan fast, and we needed to tend to other details. (For the record, no one complained about the cake, and I can't actually remember how many tiers it had.)

I hesitate to criticize those who spend eighteen months planning a wedding; it is, after all, a unique event. But the marriage celebration is a familiar example of how planning and decision time will expand like an accordion to fill the schedule we permit.

How long does it take to plan a wedding? The true answer is: it takes from now until the day before the wedding. Choosing invitations can take ten minutes or six months. How much time have you got? (The parallel question of "How much does a wedding cost?" has the same answer.)

This dynamic is not limited to weddings. How long does it take to choose a marketing vendor? To decide on a company mission statement? To set the lunch menu for a board meeting? To pick out the right outfit? To write an email message?

I don't suggest that those tasks are of equal importance; clearly they are not. But any of them could vary one-hundredfold in the time and energy they consume. Claiming "we're too busy to decide now" may not advance the issue or improve the quality of the decision, but it will certainly add time and cost to the process. If you come back to that decision again and again, revisiting it will carry a substantial cost.

Avoiding the Drama of Drawn-Out Decisions

Hamlet could have been a short play. After all, if he had believed the ghost and simply avenged Dad in Act One, well…. Thankfully, Shakespeare had a different plan—a decisive Dane would have robbed the world of great drama.

But do you want drama in your team decision-making? When a decision is postponed for busyness or any other reason, the door is opened for anyone on the team to come back to it—at virtually any time—and re-open that discussion.

Indecision, excessive debate, waffling, and vacillating are toxic to productivity. To avoid that poison, always elect one of two paths when faced with a team decision:

- **DECIDE.** Make the call of Yea or Nay, Go or No-go.

- **DECIDE TO DECIDE LATER.** Make a specific appointment in the future—choose a date and time—to revisit the decision.

Postponement can be the right path; your team may be better equipped to decide with the benefit of future information. But would you ever say, "Instead of deciding this now, let's spend twenty minutes a day thinking and talking about it for the next three months. How does that sound?" While that course would never be intentional, the issue could play out that way if you don't either reach a conclusion now or decide to resume discussion at a specific later date—and not before.

GETTING OUT OF THE TOO-BUSY TRAP

There are several familiar and proven methods of saving time that apply at home and in the workplace. As you aim to avoid being "too swamped" to take the right actions, you will want to apply each of the methods as levers to get more time and make better decisions.

LEVER 1: DELEGATION

When I chaired a peer group of twelve CEOs, four of the members were always ahead of the others. Their companies were growing and thriving, and they were able to be strategic and plan for the future. The other eight were more often called away from our meetings by staff issues or business crises and struggled to get away from hands-on problem solving at their companies. After some time, I noticed that all four of the "more successful" leaders shared a primary characteristic: they all delegated well. They had entrusted others with various functions at their companies and felt comfortable leaving those people alone.

My experience with the CEO group is not scientific proof, but numerous experts and studies have demonstrated that the skill of delegation is essential for businesses to grow, and that lack of delegation is a key reason that most companies never graduate from the small-business phase.[6]

Delegation takes time, and delegation makes time.

Whether it's a business, a church, a classroom, or a social club, the leader's time will increase as she lets others take on more responsibility. We also see this in parenting. It's time-consuming to teach children to tie shoes, use chopsticks, or do the laundry, but when the youngsters can clothe, feed, and clean themselves, the job of parenting becomes much less labor-intensive. (Not necessarily easier, but less manual work.)

Delegation doesn't just happen. It requires intent and commitment. Are you too busy to delegate to your reports, or to train your new hire, or to bring on a new vendor? If you are, then you'll probably continue to be too busy. (You also may fall behind on quality or suffer greater risk, as we explore in the discussion of the related Expensive Sentence, "We can probably do that ourselves.")

LEVER 2: PROCESS AND DOCUMENTATION

Every business, team, and family engages in many activities that are repeated. Even if you don't work at an assembly line, somewhere in your company people are conducting routine activities: paying invoices, responding to customer inquiries, writing proposals, testing software enhancements, or doing something that happens at least a few times every year. At home, we pay bills, write holiday cards, and go on trips with periodic repetition.

Without documentation or a standard process for these activities, someone will have to remember or figure out the right way to execute a task every time it's done. This takes time and can generate uneven quality and added risk. But when we have a guide, it's quicker, easier, and better. For example, whenever we follow a recipe to create a meal, we eliminate the time-consuming tasks of planning and experimenting. At the same time, we reduce the risk that something will be unsafe or unappetizing.

One of the essential phases of business maturity is shifting from personal knowledge to documented processes. Businesses that are too busy to become process-oriented remain dependent on the memory and expertise of individuals. In addition to adding cost, being too busy to add processes will limit growth and ultimately relegate some enterprises to mom-and-pop status.

LEVER 3: ORGANIZATION AND STORAGE

One of the most basic methods of saving time is keeping items where they are needed or used. This self-evident principle doesn't require our proof, but it's worth asking the question: are the supplies we need in the best place? The growing industries of office and home organization suggest that many of us believe we can do better.[7]

In considering organization, start with the activity rather than with the items. When you're processing household bills, for example, it may be better to keep bank deposit slips with stamps and envelopes rather than with other bank documents. This activity-based storage will save time and possible stress by eliminating the time to find items; it may even eliminate potential late fees with vendors. Or—to save even more time—someone may choose to handle their bills with automation and technology.

LEVER 4: AUTOMATION AND TECHNOLOGY

In a prior life, I spent my days surrounded by phone bills. I co-founded a company that processed and audited telecom invoices for large companies, and my role was leading operations. At the time, most of the bills we handled were in paper format, but we had the option of converting those bills to electronic form. This conversion was a chore. It took multiple bill cycles (i.e., months) for the carriers to receive our request, send a test invoice, and then make the final migration from paper to electronic billing. This seemed like such a hassle to me that I procrastinated on converting the bills. I told myself I was "too busy" in the daily work of processing the paper bills to invest time in the process of getting bills electronically.

So we kept working with the paper bills until the day the CEO said something along the lines of "Why the heck are we swimming in paper?" The excuse was my own busyness. That was a bad answer, as failure to make the right choice in prioritizing my time made the whole company less efficient.

Four months later, we had almost all of our large bills in electronic format. That reduced the time required to process a bill from two days to two hours, freeing up hundreds of hours a month of staff time. "I'm too swamped to deal with changing the bill format" had been a highly Expensive Sentence.

Applying the Levers to Save Time

There is nothing magical about the time-saving levers of delegation, process, organization, and automation. These steps may seem so obvious that we overlook their power to free hours in our day and add capacity to our teams. We can apply them widely.

Finding the Factories

If your workplace is a classic "flow shop"—such as an automotive assembly line or a television factory—it's obvious that every step is repeated tens of thousands of times, and any small improvement will yield a major long-term benefit. The flow shop is where operational science was born.

Process improvement can also benefit "job shops," where every project is different and the work varies. On your team, what are the activities that happen only a few times a month? Are they supported with the right documentation and technology? Wherever there is repetition, there is room for improvement.

10% × 10% Can Be a Large Number

If a full-timer spends 10 percent of her time on a particular activity, it means she is doing it four hours per week. That's 200 hours every year. If that activity can be improved by just 10 percent, that's a savings of twenty hours. If there are four people doing that same activity for 10 percent of their time, that savings would be eighty hours. Would two extra weeks be helpful to your team? Is it worth a few hours to pursue those savings?

As a guideline, consider any activity on which someone spends at least 10 percent of their time worthy of review and improvement. In fact, improving processes and applying technology can be very worthwhile for far less frequent activities—even things that we might do just a few times a month and that might take only seconds (like paying a toll on a highway).

COMBATTING THE MINDSET OF BUSYNESS

Being busy is accepted and celebrated in our culture, which makes it the perfect dodge. When your packed schedule is the reason you decline, it will be taken as a much more suitable answer than any number of actual truths:

- "I don't like you, and I'm not going to do what you say."

- "If I follow through on your suggestion, it will show how inefficient I've been."

- "I'm too lazy to figure out whether that would really help or not."

- "I don't like to delegate because I'm a control freak."

- "That sounds good but would require me to change. I fear change."

- "I'm too much of a perfectionist to take on something without completely mastering it."

While one of these responses might get you in trouble, you'll rarely be held to account with a reply of "That sounds great, but I'm too swamped." Don't accept the excuse from yourself or those on your team.

Just Saying "No'?

Claiming busyness may be an easy way to say "no." And "no" may be the right answer. It's perfectly fine to conclude that you don't want to pursue a course of action because:

1. You think it won't really help you.

2. It might cost too much money.

3. It's not a priority at the moment.

If your team makes that decision and you prefer to tell a salesperson "we're too busy" (or for that matter, "we have to wash our hair" or some other excuse), that is fine. I'm not arguing that every answer must be fully transparent. But make sure your team understands the real reasons you are saying no so that you don't deceive yourselves. Don't let your handy excuse feed the perception of busyness. It could become a bad habit.

We Become Addicted to Busy

Everyone goes through seasons of over-busyness or urgency. It may happen at a non-profit where donations have dropped 30 percent and all hands need to help out with fundraising. Perhaps it's after a company has moved offices and the team has to unpack boxes and find the restrooms while still keeping the customers satisfied. Or maybe there's a stretch when you're juggling school part-time and work full-time, and a family member has a health crisis.

Those times come, but they should also go. When the schedule ramps way up and doesn't fade back down, the problem may be more related to the person than to the circumstances.

A workaholic is defined as someone who avoids personal matters under cover of professional demands. The term "workaholic" has existed for decades, but in recent years there has been more attention and academic study on the subject of busyness addiction. What scientists appear to be learning on this subject is rather amazing: a person addicted to busyness experiences a brain response to activity that is virtually identical to that of a drug user.[8]

A Culture of Urgency

Can a group of people become addicted to being busy? In some teams, it seems like the seasons of over-packed schedules blend together to a point where it never ends.

Has your team fallen into an ongoing culture of urgency? Listen for telltale clues:

- "I'm sure that would help our company, but we just have too much on our plates right now."

- "That may be the way this industry is headed, but we're too focused on our current direction..."

- "We're not at a place where we can even think about that."

- "It's crazy-busy here."

Despite the façade of activity, research is revealing that over-busyness destroys creativity and hinders productivity.[9]

Making Decisions in Survival Mode

When the near-term future is uncertain due to a lack of resources, a team sometimes will declare itself to be in "survival mode." Survival mode implies that long-term planning is impossible because attention must be paid to getting through the near term. This is reasonable—if your family doesn't have food to eat today, you'll be forgiven for not planting a crop for next fall. But consider two warnings about survival mode:

First, beware the power of thought. When everyone on the team begins to wonder if the organization is going to survive, negative thinking can be a self-fulfilling prophecy. Leaders can be honest, and at the same time use discretion in how and with whom they share the full truth.

Second, a survival mindset can produce decisions that harm the organization. Pilots are trained that when they have emergency mechanical problems in mid-flight, there is one thing they must do first and foremost as they deal with the crisis: keep flying the airplane. Leaders have the difficult job of balancing short-term needs with long-term health, and must try to avoid sacrificing the latter because of the perceived urgency of the former.

BUSYNESS IS A CHOICE

You're Busy. I'm Busy. We are all busy.

Sometimes we need to be reminded that everyone has exactly the same amount of time, and most people believe that they spend their time in worthwhile pursuits. You are busy doing exactly what you choose to do. I say this with care, but you just might need to... get over yourself?

Our schedules may be full of important things. But if we are too busy to make the right decisions, we might dearly regret ignoring a problem that may grow and cause great harm—or an opportunity that could bring enormous benefit.

WISE REPLIES TO "WE'RE TOO SWAMPED..."

Whether prohibitive busyness is authentic or perceived, you don't want to let it become the carpet under which poor decision-making is swept. Let's turn our attention to making sure that doesn't happen.

RESPONDING DIRECTLY TO EXPENSIVE SENTENCES

An Expensive Sentence can be redirected and then used to spark a productive conversation. The next time you hear "we're too swamped to think about that now" or another version of the too-busy excuse, try tailoring one of the replies below to use with your team.

❝ *We feel swamped, but maybe we are not always focused on the most important things. My sense is that we need to look into this idea now because it could be a big part of our future."*

❝ *I'm afraid that we're too busy to get un-busy. What I mean by that is that this idea might save us time, so we can be less busy. Wouldn't that be cool?"*

❝ *We're never too busy to do the right thing. Let's spend a half-hour looking into this together, and then make a decision: 1) move forward with the change, 2) stay as we are, or 3) decide to pick this up on a specific future date and time."*

❝ *Of course we have to keep the trains running. But I'm wondering if six months from now, we might look back and wish we had taken action on this sooner."*

Departing from the Language of Busyness

If "too busy" is a common and costly excuse on your team, take it on directly. Call the team together and discuss how to apply these steps.

Step 1: Reject the Premise of Busyness

If someone were drowning nearby, would you be too busy to save them? Of course not. If the company were about to fail, would you be too busy to take action to save it? Again, no. These questions are rhetorical, but it's important to establish, articulate, and reinforce that on your team, you are not too busy to do the right thing or the smart thing.

Here are some practical suggestions to make sure your team doesn't hide under cover of being busy.

- Start a "busy jar": anyone who claims they are too busy is fined a dollar.

- Create a book club and read a book about on busyness, such as *Busy* by Tony Crabbe or *Addicted to Busy* by Brady Boyd. Then discuss whether or how it applies on your team.

- Ask those around you to tell you when you seem busy and how it affects them. (Note: this is a courageous invitation that may spark surprising feedback. Be sure you are ready to accept the candid perceptions of your team before going down this route.)

Step 2: Pivot to Priority

Is your team helplessly driven by circumstances and bandwidth, or does it strategically decide where it is headed? To take the active path, we may need to pivot from being busyness-constrained to being priority-driven.

Saying "no" is glorious when we say no to the right things and for the right reasons. But passing up a rare strategic opportunity because of a tactical backlog is a path to extinction. It's OK to de-prioritize; it's much less OK to ignore an opportunity or to claim busyness as an excuse.

After laying out options, decide what to defer or decline in the context of team priorities. Give the team permission to distinguish between good and best, between salutary and necessary. Deciding that a good thing isn't the right thing at the moment might be the best possible decision.

Step 3: Restate the Truth

Now that you have rejected the false premise of busyness and worked through your priorities, you can rewrite that Expensive Sentence with one that is far more useful.

- "We will start this customer care program now because it aligns with our mission and will allow us to be more successful."

- "Though starting a feedback program has been useful for some of our competitors, our focus is on innovation and it doesn't fit into our strategic plan."

- "It would be great to bring in a vendor to help us reduce expenses, but our CFO and finance leaders are still adjusting to the new accounting system. We'll revisit this in early March and make a go-or-no-go decision."

Note the timeframe specified in the last bullet point. If this isn't a priority now, decide when you will revisit the issue.

Exercises to Outwit Over-Busyness

As with many Expensive Sentences, the claim of being too busy usually rests on poor information and the vagaries of the unknown. With a small investment of time, your team can replace a vague guess with a structured estimate of the costs and benefits of pursuing a new idea.

Exercise: Conduct a Ten-Minute Cost-Benefit Analysis

A *cost-benefit analysis* is simply a way to organize the pros and cons of taking a specific action and assign numeric values or estimates. The steps are straightforward:

1. Brainstorm all of the different types of costs

2. Estimate amounts or ranges for the costs

3. List all the benefits

4. Ballpark the value of the benefits

5. Compare your cost estimate to your benefit estimate

Your output for this exercise may be a whiteboard with two columns and some numbers; if it is, take a picture and send it to your teammates. Or if you have notes in an email that's also fine. The analysis does not need to be perfect or comprehensive; a quick review is one hundred times better than no analysis at all.

EXERCISE: ASSESS YOUR PROBLEM OR GOAL INVENTORY

In *Same Side Selling*, Ian Altman and I write about the challenges salespeople face when confronted with buyers who are too busy and don't follow through. This is an enormous frustration for many salespeople in all fields who can't seem to hold the customer's attention long enough to make a sale.

"We're too busy" may be an excuse that a buyer passes along, but it more likely indicates that the salesperson hasn't connected his solution to a problem that the buyer believes is urgent. In Ian's words:

> It's not enough to be able to solve a problem that your buyer has. It has to be a problem that rates 8, 9, or 10 on the scale of 1–10. Anything below that, they may agree would be helpful, but they won't make a priority of buying it.[10]

The 1–10 scale is arbitrary but helpful, and it's just as useful for your own internal priorities as it is for those you are selling to. If it works better to view your objectives as "goals" that's fine; but it is often the case problems carry more urgency than goals (and many goals could be expressed as solving problems).

If the action under consideration does not solve an important problem, then you have the answer to whether or not to go forward. You are not passing because you're busy or distracted; you are making an informed decision based upon solving the problems that are most pressing.

CHAPTER 3

"WE NEED IT YESTERDAY"

"This is urgent."

"We have to act—NOW."

"Don't just stand there... do something!"

"We can't afford to wait."

ONE OF THE MOST SUCCESSFUL ADVERTISING CAMPAIGNS OF THE 1980S featured an unlikely subject. The commercials didn't promote a beer, a snack, a toy, or any sort of consumer product. Instead, the star was a freight company. The tagline brilliantly summed up the company's function, purpose, and brand: "Federal Express. When it absolutely, positively has to be there overnight."

The company blanketed weekend sporting events with television ads and became a household name. Yet its success would depend on how businesses and consumers answered a key question: how often does a shipped item have to arrive overnight?

Absolutely?

Positively?

The company founder, Fred Smith, believed that there was a latent desire for faster shipping and that people would pay a premium for it. When Smith first proposed the idea in term paper at Yale, his professor failed to see its potential and gave him an average grade.[11]

We know how this story went. Federal Express (which shortened its name to FedEx in 1994) enjoyed spectacular growth and became as integral to many businesses as the telephone or regular mail. In the business world and beyond, more and more people developed the expectation that something mailed today should arrive tomorrow. Of course, in some parts of life waiting even one day has become unacceptable.

OUR GROWING NEED FOR SPEED

A friend of mine shared of a recent vacation with his family. His four-year-old daughter asked if she could watch *Dora the Explorer* on the hotel TV. Dad explained that Dora might not be on right now, and after checking the channels they learned this was the case. The poor girl didn't understand how Dora could not be available. At home, Dora was on TV whenever she wanted it. She wanted Dora. Now.

At the risk of sounding prehistoric, this author was raised on television before the days of the video recorder—either digital or VHS. Either you watched a TV show at the specific time it was broadcast, or you missed it. When the ability to capture programming on videotape (and thereby watch it whenever you wanted) first entered widespread culture, it was revolutionary. But today that revolution is as distant culturally as the American Revolution is distant historically. It is now unfathomable that we cannot access our favorite programs whenever we want. (In fact, rereading this paragraph reveals several terms that are rather outdated: VHS, tape, "missing" a show, broadcast... maybe even television.)

AN ON-DEMAND, OVER-CAFFEINATED WORLD

Shipping and entertainment are not the only areas where the pace has changed. We can see how virtually every corner of our lives moves to a faster drumbeat. We've filled our kitchens with precooked lasagna noodles and pre-mixed smoothies. Decorating a home used to take months. Then came 2-Day Blinds, and after that standard was set, it had to be surpassed with Next Day Blinds. (I guess the next steps are Blinds Today and then... Blinds Yesterday?)

The point of calling attention to our on-demand world—and the fact that it hasn't always been that way—is to consider how our thinking has been shaped. We have been trained to believe that we need it now. But we might not really need it—whatever "it" is—right now.

We can also see the pattern in which yesterday's luxuries become today's necessities. It wasn't that long ago that we didn't have everything overnight. Our species muddled through for a few thousand years. Then overnight service became first available, then widely used, and then expected.

When we realize that we didn't always require such speed, we might ask: Why are we in such a hurry anyway? Are we truly stuck in a situation in which we have to act right away?

WHEN WE GET PULLED INTO URGENCY

The philosophical questions are worth asking, and later in this chapter we'll present practical questions to examine urgency. But in the real world urgency isn't always our choice. Even if we adopt more patience in our personal expectations, the people and circumstances around us will foist urgency upon us. It may look like one of these scenes:

- A client threatens to leave you, claiming your software is too slow

- A new project is scheduled to start next week, but you don't have the staff in place to handle it

- A good friend tells you that his marriage is in trouble

- Your child pronounces that she hates being in band and wants to quit

These cases present more than a superficial preference for speed. They are real problems that could get worse if something does not change. Yet a mindset of "we need it yesterday" or "we have to fix this NOW" won't necessarily be the best approach. Consider these reactive instant responses:

- Client threatens: You offer a sharp discount to win back the customer, or you hastily invest in a solution that you hope will improve your system speed.

- Understaffed: You rush to hire someone who can do the work, or you tell your client that you cannot accept the new project.

- Troubled Marriage: You offer specific relationship advice to your friend.

- Unhappy Child: You tell your child that she can quit band.

These actions might help. Then again, it's easy to imagine that any one of these reactive steps might fail to solve the real problem, which might then repeat not too far in the future.

THE COST OF URGENCY

When we are cornered and forced to respond, we can. But that response may not be the best course. Whether it's taking the wrong turn on the highway, performing an unneeded surgical procedure, choosing the wrong vendor, or marrying the wrong person, urgency can lead to decisions that we regret.

Compromised Decision-Making

Let's consider the specific ways in which urgency degrades decisions:

- **URGENCY REDUCES OPTIONS.** All options fit into one of three buckets: 1) do something now; 2) wait now and do something later; or 3) don't do anything. From this perspective, urgency wipes away two entire categories of response as it insists on immediate action. Moreover, a need for speed means that even prompt action that doesn't bring instant results may be discounted or eliminated outright. Speed dominates to the exclusion of other factors and features.

- **URGENCY DESTROYS BARGAINING POWER.** One of the classic techniques in negotiation is to run out the clock when the other side is on a strict schedule. If we must start implementation next week, then we don't have the option of negotiating for another week or of taking time to develop alternatives. This will impact not just the price we pay but the quality of our results. For this reason, we should be especially wary of urgency when we are in any type of negotiation or purchase, and be cognizant that the other side may attempt to create urgency for us. It is worth noting the extent to which modern marketers use (and abuse!) the premise of urgency. From online offers that expire at midnight, to one-day-only sales, to claims of limited inventory and pricing that is valid only if you call in the next ten minutes, those trying to sell to us depend on urgency to hasten our buying decisions.

- **URGENCY KILLS PROCESS.** Urgency dictates a path that does not tolerate deliberative review. If your process requires three bids or multiple reference checks, urgency may tempt you to skip those safeguards. When the right stakeholders are not involved or the appropriate evaluation phase is skipped, the decision is likely to suffer.

- **URGENCY SELF-REPLICATES.** As we referenced earlier, urgent items create more urgency when they push important items from the agenda… until they become urgent. This potential spiral makes it even more important to recognize urgency and arrest it when it is not useful.

Despite these headwinds, it is possible to make good decisions under urgent circumstances. It would be akin to writing an email while someone is screaming at you, or doing hard math immediately after dropping a hammer on your toe. Possible, but difficult. Urgency screams and throbs and says "do something now," prioritizing any action over the best action.

Conversely, an absence of urgency affords multiple luxuries. With more time, we can make a better-quality decision and we have more options available to us. Let's consider how less-urgent remedies might apply to our scenarios:

- Client threatens: You schedule a face-to-face meeting with the client to make sure you understand their concerns. Meanwhile, you conduct a study to measure the speed of your system versus the competition, and begin evaluating ways to effectively increase speed.

- Understaffed: You investigate whether the project could be delayed somewhat without penalty, and you begin a careful search for the right new hire.

- Troubled Marriage: You spend more time listening to your friend, and perhaps meet with the spouse as well. Or you connect them to marriage counselors.

- Unhappy Child: You empathize with your child and assure them that you want the best, but agree not to make any decisions while she is upset. You schedule a time to talk about the issue over the weekend and at that time make a plan.

Added Cost

Even if we manage to make good decisions under the gun, there are likely to be direct financial costs for getting the solution as soon as possible. We know that overnight shipping costs more than regular mail, sometimes by a factor of ten or twenty. That premium can be money well spent when speed is required, but often it is needless cost.

Freight isn't the only field in which speed costs more, and cost is not limited to the financial realm. The impact of speed on other factors is showcased in the classic consulting paradigm that presents three dimensions of a project:

- Quality

- Scope

- Speed

The client must decide which two are most important. The implicit understanding is that—for a given price—only two dimensions can be prioritized, and the third will suffer. If you do a job with excellent quality and wide scope, it will take more time. When speed is the priority, then either quality or scope must be compromised.

If you remove the budget constraint and demand all three dimensions, you can probably pay more and get what you want. But in one way or another, speed carries a premium.

Responding Instead of Reacting

Before we accept an inferior decision or the added costs brought on by "we need it yesterday," we can take steps to validate and even reduce urgency. Our measured actions can raise the chances for a better decision, even while we respect the concerns and urgent perspective of others. (We don't have to adopt a detached, Spock-like cool or tell everyone around us to "just settle down.")

Urgent Empathy, Deliberate Action

There is an important difference between reflecting the seriousness of a situation and reacting in haste. When a colleague, friend, or family member shares a problem that they believe is urgent, it won't help to downplay their concern. In fact, it's fair to say that there is an urgent need to acknowledge those situations and express empathy. Whether it is personal pain or a threat to business success, making sure that others know you understand the gravity of the matter is important to do, and promptly.

The reason it is so important to quickly show empathy is not just to prove that you're not a callous jerk (though that is a good reason). Signaling that you care and acknowledge the issue can meaningfully reduce the perception of urgency from the other person. It can lower the temperature enough so that a better decision might be made. The converse is also true: being skeptical or dismissive of another person's concern may cause that concern to intensify.

In customer service, this power of acknowledgement to reduce perceived urgency is intuitive. Can you recall a recent experience when you complained about something in a store, restaurant, or coffee shop? How did the first person respond to you, and how did it make you feel? If you were quickly validated in your concern, you probably feel good about where things ended. If your perspective was challenged or minimized, there's a much higher chance that the establishment lost a customer.

Starbucks teaches the LATTE method for handling a customer problem. LATTE is an acronym in which the L stands for "listen" and the A means "acknowledge." These two steps precede T, for "take action." Here's the useful takeaway: the first step in handling a complaint is not to fix the problem, but to communicate properly. (So I don't leave you with a half-filled cup, the second T is a reminder to "Thank the customer" and the E to "Encourage" the customer to share any further concerns.)[12]

While it's ill-advised to thoughtlessly react to shouts of "we need it yesterday," it also won't help to dismiss them. Acknowledging the concern behind urgency is often the best way to reduce the urgency and begin a thoughtful process of how to act.

THE FIRST QUESTIONS TO ASK

An urgent situation may not feel like being stuck, because it demands action. But when the need to act now confines us to poor options, we are stuck. Action is not the same as progress toward our goals. Before making any decisions or taking any actions to solve an urgent problem, we can ask some initial questions.

- **WHAT'S THE REAL PROBLEM?** Urgency presents us with an immediate need, but that may not be the biggest need. Even when urgency demands action—when there is a literal or figurative fire to put out—the source of the problem may be something else. The child may hate band because another student was being mean to her; the client may be threatening to leave because of budget pressure; the company may be understaffed because its fees are too low to adequately hire. The initial stated problem is not always the most important problem to address.

- **IS IT *YOUR* PROBLEM?** When you get to the real issue, it's important to consider who actually owns it. An unhappy client or spouse presents a good occasion for introspection. But it does not necessarily mean that something needs to change on our part. Those of us that are high-empathy solver types need to be especially cautious about taking on problems that may belong to someone else.

- **WILL ACTION HELP SOLVE THE PROBLEM?** One of my favorite prods to action is the advice that "you cannot steer a car when it's parked." Slightly less helpful is the demand, "Don't just stand there, do something." These sayings reveal a bias toward outward action that is natural: when we act, we feel like we are doing something productive. But when we force action on a situation where it doesn't help, these intended encouragements can become Expensive Sentences.

Defining the real problem, who owns it, and whether action will help may take some time. We may need to remind ourselves that if we don't take time to think the matter through now we may have even less time in the future.

A perceived lack of time is at the heart of "we need it yesterday," just as it was with the phrase "we're too swamped for that now." While the prior chapter's Expensive Sentence causes us to postpone and delay action, this one may lead us to move too quickly. Before we let that thinking sabotage our success, we can determine whether the urgency is valid or if we might have more time.

FOUR QUESTIONS TO CROSS-EXAMINE URGENCY

As with most Expensive Sentences, "we need it yesterday" is most potent in the abstract. The specific answers to four questions will reveal whether we really need something right now or would be better served to wait.

QUESTION 1: WHOSE DEADLINE IS IT, ANYWAY?

The schedules on our calendars and in our minds came from somewhere. Remembering the origin of that deadline can help us determine how legitimate it is.

When I was younger, I had an idea that I wanted to be married by a certain age. When that year came and went, I was still single. Life went on, and thankfully I did not succumb to false urgency in this most important arena of life and marry the wrong person. (But it has been done, hasn't it?)

When we question urgency, the first step is to ask where the time-frame came from. Was it a commitment to another party? Is there an external event or dependency? Did someone throw it out in an email as a guess? Or is the deadline driven by our own internal sense of the right timing?

If the source is not external, we should be aware of the strong bias of *anchoring*. Whatever we saw as a first impression or the most recent example of an event may be imprinted deeply as a default standard, whether or not it should be.

- If Mom had her first child at twenty-eight, then we should too; right?

- Uncle Vince went to business school right after college, so isn't that the best time to go?

- The last product launch took eight weeks; shouldn't this one be the same?

- The VP referenced that we were going to start the program this month, so we have to, right?

Sometimes simply identifying the source of the deadline is freeing because we realize that our timeframe is arbitrary and easily changed. Even if the deadline is valid, knowing its source allows us to analyze it further.

QUESTION 2: WHAT COULD BE GAINED BY WAITING?

Barring a valid reason to postpone action, it's better to move right away. But waiting with a specific intention can improve decisions. Here are some valid reasons to pause:

- **GATHERING INFORMATION** — If we are collecting data or consulting with others, then a delay could put us in a better position to decide. There should be specific expectations for both the timelines and the information: "let's talk to the customer tomorrow and make sure that the system speed was the real reason they left" or "when we get the test results back next week we'll know more."

- **LETTING OTHERS ACT** — If responsibility for the matter is not completely clear, we might see how others respond to a situation. Examples: "Before we file a complaint let's see if they announce a policy change" or "our customer might see this as their issue, so let's give them some time to respond before we take action."

- **EXPECTING ADDITIONAL OPTIONS** — Solutions on the horizon might be better suited to address the issue. If better technology or smarter experts are arriving soon, the fastest path to a good outcome might be a short-term wait: "Before we build a workaround, let's see if the new software release is compatible" or "the new manager starting next week might be the perfect person to own this project."

It's also possible that if you wait, the perceived urgent issue will simply fade away. But real problems don't often solve themselves, and it's not a good policy to postpone action out of pure hope that things will get better. Hope supported by a likelihood that one of the bullet points above will change circumstances is a stronger rationale.

QUESTION 3: HOW MUCH TIME WOULD MAKE A DIFFERENCE?

When "we need it yesterday" is the prevailing mood on a team, any mere suggestion of any delay might seem treasonous. But certainly there is a difference between a one-hour delay, a one-week delay, and a one-year delay… isn't there? Before you conclude that you can't delay, consider the length of delay that is likely.

Defining the time requires us to put a schedule on the factors we identified in the last question:

- When are we going to have more information?

- When might others act? How long are we willing to wait for them to act?

- When will more options present themselves?

- What would have to happen that might remove our need to take action? When could we reasonably expect that to happen?

QUESTION 4: WHAT IS THE COST OF DELAY?

In spy movies and international dramas, the implicit threat behind urgency is destruction. Fans of the show 24 can recall the voice of Jack Bauer demanding, "Dammit, Chloe, I need it now!" Failure to get the job done would mean bombs exploding and innocent people dying.

First responders, medical professionals, and those in the law and intelligence communities may face life-or-death urgency in the course of their jobs. For most of us, the stakes are lower. So let's say things are delayed: the project slips by two weeks; the new hire starts in July instead of May; the luncheon isn't held until next month. How would that actually affect the cost and results?

Understanding the true costs of delay, we can weigh them against the costs of acting too quickly.

FINDING THE FEAR

We take people to urgent care or the emergency room because we fear that their medical condition might get worse without prompt attention. Indeed, urgency is often driven by fear. Sometimes a rush to action is fully appropriate—especially if someone's health or safety is at risk. But in other cases, we may be misled by the old acronym FEAR: False Evidence Appearing Real.

Whether the threat is real or imagined, fear distorts decision-making by magnifying those things we want to avoid. Just as with other types of emotion or bias, it's not realistic to think that we can remove fear completely from our thinking. Our goal should be first to discern whether fear is driving us, then to identify what it is that we fear and why we fear it. At that point, we may be able to analyze the possible negative outcomes rationally and make a better decision.

Early in my career I shared about a possible job change with a mentor. He asked me "Are you running to something, or are you running from something?" The question cut to the heart of my motivation. It spurred me to consider whether the new job was really something that I wanted for the right reasons, after careful deliberation and searching, or whether I was acting out of fear: the urgent belief that I needed to change things now. When we can't clearly define a positive reason for an action, it's more likely that we are driven by fear.

It helps to be aware of some of the most common types of fear that drive urgency.

- **FEAR OF LOSS.** If we have the sense that we might lose a customer, suffer a financial loss, or lose access to a tool or relationship that we enjoy, the fear of losing something can spur us to take action quickly. The fear of loss can be just as strong when its target is something we don't have yet: a job candidate who may take another offer, a sale that ends tomorrow, or the opportunity to snag a large business deal.

- **FEAR OF MISSING OUT.** This fear has its own catchy acronym: FOMO. Its context is often social media, but I believe that this version of peer pressure shows up on teams as well. Some company leaders feel compelled to use a specific technology, attend a respected industry event, obtain a certain type of customer, or take some other urgent action to stay competitive or maintain the desired image. If there is not a specific potential loss at hand, then fear might be driven by the vague negative of "missing out" on something worthwhile.

- **FEAR OF DISAPPOINTING OTHERS.** People-pleasers are sometimes driven to urgency because they don't want to disappoint someone. It's worth noting that the "someone" may be prominent in the person's life (a spouse, a boss, or a parent) or a person they have never met (like an audience member at a public speaking event, or an online reviewer). This fear might appear as performance anxiety, or the fear of being unprepared or of losing one's reputation.

Any one of these fears can be valid. Legitimate fears help us focus on genuine danger or risk and can motivate us to work harder. But it always helps to define fear as specifically as possible. Undefined fear often becomes outsized and clouds our judgment with misplaced urgency.

STRATEGIC PATIENCE: THE UPSIDE OF WAITING

Speed is a matter of perspective. Maybe you've heard the story of the snail that was mugged by two turtles. When the policeman asked for a statement, the victimized snail was stumped: "Gosh, it all happened so fast…."

Recurring urgency may reveal a bias toward short-term thinking. Is your team oriented toward this month's targets or a five-year vision? Leadership requires both long-term thinking and short-term action. If a team understands the big picture and is confident about long-term direction, it is less likely that false urgency can derail decisions. On the other hand, if everyone thinks that the future of the company depends on this month's sales, a sense of urgency can be more likely to dominate.

"Speed to market" and "first-mover advantage" imply an importance in moving quickly. But while it's sometimes true that the first entrant into a field has an advantage, trailblazers often face a difficult path. The term "bleeding edge" describes companies and products that pioneer a field but don't enjoy business success. (Financial losses constitute the "bleeding.") History provides many examples in which the trailblazers suffered as later comers thrived. Here are a few that may be familiar:

- Zantac was not the first effective ulcer drug, but had fewer side effects than others on the market and became the best-selling prescription drug in the world.

- Apple did not invent the MP3 player, but they revised the product and dominated the category with the iPod.

- Google entered a crowded field of search engines, and ultimately surpassed all of them.

When a new technology or concept enters the marketplace, there can be a substantial period of time before it reaches wide adoption and large sales volumes which allow for profitability. In contrast, later entrants have distinctive advantages. They don't have to educate consumers on what their product is, they can learn from the mistakes of other companies, and they can take advantage of newer technologies without needing to transition from outdated production. If our urgency is driven by a desire to be the first ones at the party, it's worth remembering that the later guests often have more fun.

WISE REPLIES TO "WE NEED IT YESTERDAY"

Let's review sample language, conversation topics, and exercises to reduce the impact of false urgency on your team.

RESPONDING DIRECTLY TO EXPENSIVE SENTENCES

The next time you hear "we need it yesterday" or "we have to act now," engage in discussion with your team using some of the language below:

❝ *This might be helpful, but we don't want to rush. We didn't have it yesterday, we don't have it now, and we are OK. I'm not saying I'm against it, but I am against going into this without the right process."*

❝ *I'm with you; it feels like we need this product immediately. But what is the actual cost of waiting an extra two weeks so we can look into other solutions and make sure we're getting the right price? How much will it cost us in time and in missed opportunities?"*

❝ *We don't want to delay a decision for no reason, but would we have more information if we did slow down a bit? Is it possible that we won't even need this at all if things go in a certain direction?"*

❝ *Let's pause for a minute; we've learned that we don't always make the best decisions when we are in a hurry."*

CONVERSATION TOPICS

Trying to go fast will often have the opposite effect. We're familiar with this principle and have many ways to say it. When is the last time you heard one of these expressions on your team?

Haste makes waste.

Shortcuts can slow us down.

Measure twice, cut once.

Slow is smooth, smooth is fast.

The right way is the fast way.

Other familiar warnings remind us that there are no quick fixes, no crash diets with lasting results, and no silver bullets that will instantly solve thorny problems. Does your team act like you believe these sayings? In what settings are these cautions true, and when are they not true?

These additional questions may help your team identify false urgency:

- Where do we need to act quickly on our team? Where is it better to act with more deliberation?

- Let's consider some of the decisions we have made in the last year: hiring employees, engaging vendors, new projects, responding to customers. How was the decision-making process? Is there any chance we acted too quickly or rashly?

- Are there times when pursuing speed has actually slowed us down?

- What are we afraid of on our team? Competitors? Lack of funds? How are those fears serving us? How are they affecting us in a negative way?

EXERCISES TO AVOID FALSE URGENCY

Instead of settling for vague and Expensive Sentences such as "we have to act now" or "we can't afford to wait," you can define the reasons for urgency and estimate the actual cost of waiting.

EXERCISE: DOCUMENT THE IMPACT OF WAITING

Define the source of urgency by simply writing down the impact of delay. Use a simple bullet point list and begin every item with the word "might" or the word "will" to show whether the outcome is certain or not. Include both positive and negative outcomes. The sentence may look like this:

If we don't make a decision on our marketing vendor this week, we...

- *Might find a better partner and save money*

- *Will not be able to start the fall campaign this month*

- *Might not be able to get the ad placements we are hoping for*

Putting any problem on paper often has the effect of making it seem more manageable. In just a few minutes the potential benefit and cost of delay will be more clear.

EXERCISE: DEFINE THE COST OF WAITING WITH EXPECTED VALUE

An excellent tool to assess the cost of waiting is an expected value calculation. This requires three components:

- Any possible negative outcomes that could be caused by a delay

- The likelihood of the negative outcomes

- The cost of the negative outcomes

We don't like to wait because bad things might happen. This exercise is a structured way to answer: What bad things might happen, how likely are they to happen, and how bad are they?

To illustrate, let's walk through the example of the client who threatens to leave your company because of slow software. We'll assume that the team agrees on the need to improve system speed, but while some are saying "we have to act now"—perhaps with a known vendor and product that would increase network capacity—other voices are recommending that the team shop around and consider other solutions.

The first step to define the cost of waiting is to list the negative outcomes that might occur. After brainstorming, the team agrees on this list:

1. The company could lose Customer A who threatened to leave

2. The company could lose a second customer for the same reason

3. The slow software might deter a potential customer from signing up

The next step is to assign a likelihood to each of these potential events. We'll assume for this example that the complaining customer is serious, and the team sees the likelihood of their departure at fifty percent if action is not taken immediately. It's less likely that a customer who hasn't threatened will leave, so the team assigns that probability at 20%. Finally, the team acknowledges that there is some possibility a prospect might choose a competitor because the competitor's software is faster, but this is only a small part of the purchase decision so the likelihood is set at 10%.

Now we have three potential events and their likelihood:

1. Customer A leaves   50%

2. Another customer leaves   20%

3. A prospect doesn't buy   10%

The third step is to assign a financial value to each event. Our illustration is simple because each outcome is either getting or losing a customer, and we'll say that the company values each customer as contributing $10,000 to the company's profits annually. (Warning: you can get very sophisticated in determining customer value, and rightly so, but for this exercise we don't need to be precise or perfect. The point here is to come up with a number that is pretty close to the truth.) So pegging customer value at $10,000, we can now find the expected value of each of these negative consequences:

1. Customer A leaves   50% × $10,000 = $5,000

2. Another customer leaves   20% × $10,000 = $2,000

3. A prospect doesn't buy   10% × $10,000 = $1,000

The events are independent—meaning that all three could possibly happen, and any one event happening doesn't impact the other possible events—so we find the expected value of waiting by adding up all three. In this case, that number is $8,000.

Now that we have defined the cost of waiting with a number that we can explain and defend, we are far better positioned to decide our course. If the remedy pushed by the "act now!" crowd cost $100,000 and the take-it-slow folks believe they can shop around and save at least twenty percent on the solution, we can simply compare that forecast savings ($20K) to the cost of waiting ($8K) and we have our answer.

Every step toward specificity will make it more likely that you will decide based on reason and reality instead of fear and urgency.

PART 2

REJECTING THE
SPECIAL MYTHS

THERE IS A SHORT PHRASE THAT IS WIDELY CONSIDERED THE MOST dangerous sentence in the world of finance. It's not an admonition to buy or sell. It's not a stock tip or a get-rich-quick idea, and it doesn't refer to any markets or products. It's just four simple words:

This time is different.

As harmless as those words sound, experts and historians agree that the belief behind the words has led to untold financial upheaval and market turmoil. In a book titled *This Time Is Different*, authors Carmen Reinhart and Kenneth Rogoff examine "eight centuries of financial folly": banking panics, government defaults, and massive inflationary cycles. The book explains that prior to major crises—including the most recent—a large number of people bought into the dangerous expensive sentence "this time is different."

Why is different so dangerous? If circumstances don't conform to the past, then lessons from the past don't apply. Investors have implicit permission to discard time-validated principles. Instead of acting rationally, people act as if the future will not conform to experience and proven market rules. When enough financial decision-makers follow this reckless course, it can disrupt world economies.

The dangers of believing things are different transcend macroeconomics. In this section, we will explore a parallel belief that can do just as much harm: the idea that someone or something is special.

"Special" denotes something that is rare and valuable. But like the phrase "this time is different," a designation of special can cause us to waive the principles that guide ordinary people in ordinary circumstances. When people are considered to be above or apart from others, they are excused from common standards. Whether we apply these exceptions to others or to ourselves, they bring risk and cost.

Are you special? Do you work with someone who's unique? Are you facing circumstances different from those anyone else has ever seen?

The Special myths are all around us, littering our daily lives with would-be exceptions and exemptions. Here, we'll examine three of the most hazardous myths:

- "We're different."

- "We trust them."

- "That's the way we've always done things."

"We're different" twists the reality of uniqueness into the myth that rules don't apply or that circumstances prevent a person or group from doing more.

"We trust them" reflects good intentions but can lead to imprudence, sometimes with devastating consequences.

"That's the way we've always done it" subtly asserts that the way of the past is the best way, and excuses our actions from critical evaluation.

We'll see how this myth can hurt a team terribly, even when no one says it out loud.

The Special myths are especially sly, playing on our legitimate desires and hopes. We're taught that being special is a good thing. Indeed, being different from others can sometimes help us succeed. But when the label of special is misapplied, it can isolate us and imprison us.

Let's make sure the Special myths don't become Expensive Sentences in our lives.

CHAPTER 4

"WE'RE DIFFERENT"

"That won't work for us."

"It would be nice if we could do that,
but we can't because of...."

"I have my own way of doing things."

"That could never happen to us."

Did your mother tell you that you were special?

Don't worry, I'm not going to pick on Mom, and of course you are special. You are a unique human being. There's nobody else just like you.

Now that we have that settled, let's consider some additional truths. You have to follow the rules just like everyone else, and the principles that apply to others also apply to you. In those ways, you really aren't so special.

There's a balance between the reality of being unique and the reality of being just like everybody else. When an individual loses this balance and believes that his uniqueness separates him from others, it causes problems ranging from mild self-absorption and denial to unbridled entitlement or narcissism.

The same dual reality faces teams. Each team is a collection of individuals, each of whom is unique. The team has specific strengths and assets by virtue of the people on the team and the way they work together. The team may face particular circumstances or challenges on the path to its goals.

Emphasizing a team's uniqueness, however, can be a problem. Believing that "we're different" often keeps a team looking inward instead of outward and means that standard rules don't apply. It also can provide license to work inefficiently. We might even amend that perilous phrase "this time is different" from the field of investing, and note that "this *team* is different" can bring its own costs and dangers.

Most of us have seen challenges in the office when a person or team decides they are different:

- A division at your company resists adopting the new enterprise software because "it doesn't work for them."

- A salesperson won't track leads the way his boss wants, because he has his own system.

- A VP making an expensive purchase won't follow policy and get three bids because she has special requirements.

- A manager disregards the training he received from an outside consultant because "they don't understand our industry."

These self-proclaimed exceptions can be financially costly and erode efficiency. They can also be pretty annoying to other team members, who may be tempted to say, "What's wrong, buddy? You think you're special?"

That brings us back to Mom.

The Pros and Cons of Being Different

Mom was onto something. It's not just that every person is worthy of value, though that is certainly true. Mom may have known that only by understanding uniqueness and embracing it could anyone offer their greatest contribution to the world.

The importance of differentiation has been documented extensively in business.[13] Being different is a way to innovate, to be noticed, and to stand apart from competition. At the same time, there are some areas where it's probably better to follow the herd.

A Tale of Two Differents: Quiznos Sandwiches

Have you ever eaten a Quiznos sandwich? They are tasty, but harder to find than they once were.

Quiznos was started in Colorado by a chef who created recipes for gourmet toasted sandwiches. In the 1990s, Quiznos began an aggressive franchising program, resulting in over 5,000 stores operating in 2007. That growth put Quiznos among the hottest restaurant chains in the world. However, in the next few years, more than 3,000 Quiznos stores closed, and the company was forced to declare bankruptcy in 2014. The story of Quiznos' rise and fall illustrates how being different can both help and hurt.

It was different-tasting sandwiches that fueled Quiznos' growth. Legions of fans preferred the oven-toasted flavors, which were unlike what other sandwich shops offered. Quiznos' distinctive name and fresh styling attracted customers who valued a novel alternative to fast food. Being different was central to Quiznos' success.

However, another flavor of different emerged in how the company was run. Quiznos management appeared to believe that they were different from other similar companies. Despite the benefit of following a half-century of successful fast-food chains, Quiznos did not adopt best practices in franchising. They required franchisees to buy food and supplies from them at above-market prices. Management launched a one-million-sandwich giveaway as a marketing campaign without the approval of its stores, many of which refused to honor the coupons. The corporate office allegedly withheld financial information from their franchisees. Franchisees failed at a rate four times higher than that of Subway stores.[14]

Another challenge for the stores was pricing. The Quiznos sandwiches were positioned as premium and priced higher than rival chains' subs. Because the sandwiches were different, Quiznos leadership believed their customers would pay more. This pricing philosophy proved to be a burden, especially when the recession of 2008–2009 hit. Other chains responded. Subway—on the suggestion of one of their franchisees—began offering a five-dollar foot-long sandwich, which became a huge growth driver for value-conscious customers.

Meanwhile, the competition was adapting. It made perfect sense for Quiznos' marketing campaigns to emphasize the sandwiches' toasty goodness when that was a genuine difference, but they didn't seem to plan for the fact that other sandwich chains could also buy toasters. When toasted subs began appearing at Subway, Potbellys, Firehouse Subs, and other chains, the key differentiator for Quiznos began to fade.

The saga of Quiznos illustrates how being different can help in some ways and hurt in others. Even as they tried to differentiate and beat their competitors, Quiznos would have been better off modeling their practices more closely after other successful franchise restaurants. Being different is like a fire: when controlled, it provides energy for cooking and heating. When it's not contained, it can burn down the house. It's critical to note the boundaries of that fireplace and keep different where it belongs.

THE COST OF ISOLATION

We can acknowledge that every person is unique and every company is unique. So it's not the reality of differences that cause problems, it is how we let differences shape our thoughts and actions. Those that believe that their situation lacks any meaningful connection or similarity to that of others may naturally conclude that others cannot understand them. This leads to a state of seclusion and isolation.

Isolation is dangerous. In mental illness, it can emerge as narcissism or a messianic complex. We have seen historical chapters where some believed their ethnic group to be different in a way that is above others, leading to attempted genocide. These examples are extreme, but they show the unhealthy effects that follow when humans separate themselves from others.

Even in small doses, isolation can steal practical benefits that can help us succeed. One of the joys of *not* being different is that you can learn from others who have gone before you. If your goal is to be a better math student, bake a soufflé, or learn a guitar solo, you can access the experience of the respective experts in those fields to improve.

On the other hand, if you view your path as completely new, then no one is farther along than you are. This is likely to limit perceived opportunities to learn and grow. When you last heard someone claim to be different, was the claim provided as justification? It might have been:

- A reason not to adopt best practices or new technologies

- Dismissal of an outside advice that could be useful

- A defense of why something can't get fixed or be improved

- An excuse for lower-quality service

- Reluctance to acknowledge a competitive threat

Any claims of "they don't understand our business" or "it won't work here" or "that can't happen to us" are likely to correlate with a team that is slow to learn or that fears change. Those teams will probably be left behind.

THE COST OF COMPLEXITY

Apart from the perils of isolation and stagnation, there are practical realities that can make differences expensive. These are related to basic operational principles that we encounter in business and in daily life.

If you have ever prepared school lunches for multiple children, you understand that complexity adds cost. When you can make two lunches (or three or four) that are exactly the same, the job is straightforward. It's a different story when one youngster demands peanut butter and honey, another takes only strawberry jelly, someone eats cucumbers only if the skins are cut off, and a fourth kid won't tolerate carrots. The special-order scenario adds numerous costs, as the parent has to:

- Remember the different orders,

- Maintain more food inventory on hand,

- Take extra prep time to get the added components out of the refrigerator,

- Use more time to assemble the food, and

- Shoulder the logistical burden of getting each lunch in the right bag.

SETUP COST AND INCREMENTAL COST

The economic principles at work here are *setup cost* and *incremental cost*. Any task as simple as making a peanut butter and jelly sandwich requires some setup: you need to clear an area on the counter, get out a knife and spoon, and pull the ingredients out of the pantry. Even before that, you had to acquire the ingredients at the market and also obtain the knowledge of how to make this type of sandwich. (At some point we had to learn how to make a peanut butter and jelly sandwich.) These are all setup costs.

Then we can make a sandwich. If we want to make a second peanut butter sandwich, there are no additional setup costs—we just grab bread and spread. We have the incremental cost of our time of assembly and the extra ingredients, but that's it. In fact, our instincts tell us that making five or six sandwiches wouldn't take much longer than making just one. That is, as long as it was the same kind of sandwich.

But if we change directions and need to make a turkey sandwich, we must slam the brakes on this efficient peanut butter sandwich production machine. We have to clean the counter, get new utensils, different ingredients from the refrigerator, and use a different process to make the sandwich. These are all new setup costs.

Operational costs and setup costs figure into virtually every activity, but their share of the cost varies depending on the complexity of the task, the cost of labor, the cost of materials, and how many times the activity is performed. The reason a single customized polo shirt might cost one amount, but an order of ten would be half the cost per shirt is not because of the cloth required, it's because of the setup costs.

In the abstract we always want to minimize setup costs, because setup costs are inherently non-productive. When we're preparing to make a sandwich, we're not actually making a sandwich. The same is true if we're getting ready to mow the lawn, or preparing to make sales calls, or setting up an assembly line to assemble automobiles.

Someday, my children may appreciate the sound economic policy behind their fate to eat the same lunch every day. I hope they can see how this principle plays out in every facet of life: more complexity brings more cost. Of course, the food we serve our family isn't designed to be as low-cost as possible; the goal of economy is balanced with nutrition, variety, and taste.

For many activities on your team, customization and quality may be more important than achieving the lowest possible cost. But there will be some areas where standard policies, practices, and tools will greatly reduce both cost and risk.

The Savings of Simplicity: Southwest Airlines

The flip side to complexity's cost is another important truth: simplicity brings savings. One of the great business stories in the last fifty years is Southwest Airlines. Southwest attracts attention for its fun culture, its appeal to travelers who traditionally wouldn't use airlines, and its focus on second-tier airports. However, one of the reasons that Southwest has been profitable for decades when the rest of the industry hasn't made money is its operational simplicity.

From its start, Southwest has flown only one model of airplane: the Boeing 737. While its competitors may use many different types of planes to accommodate the length and popularity of specific routes, Southwest has only one. It may seem like a small detail to use only one type of plane, but the result is a plethora of economies:

- Because Southwest pilots must be trained to fly just that one type of plane, training time and costs are reduced.

- Southwest attendants are always instantly familiar with the layout of the planes.

- The cleaning crews that turn the planes around between flights know exactly where things are and encounter little variety. The same is true for the baggage handlers.

These conveniences add up to many saved hours of labor.[15]

THE COST OF EXCEPTIONS

The team that claims "we're different" claims exception. "Your process and system might work for those other guys, but not here." Perhaps there are valid reasons to allow an exception. But by definition, exceptions create additional setup costs and bring more costs.

Reducing Exceptions to Reduce Cost

Years ago I visited the mail facility that handled all incoming payments for Capital One, which at the time was the largest bulk mailer in the country. (An executive at the company told me that Capital One accounted for 13 percent of all U.S. mail that year. I could never validate that figure, but if you remember going to the mailbox in the late 1990s, that might seem about right to you.)

The manager at the mail facility explained that he saw his job as "perpetual sub-setting." His team would divide all correspondence into certain classes and create a process for each class. When a letter didn't fit into a defined class, it was tagged as an exception. The exceptions would then be reviewed to see what classes emerged from those pieces. Again, each class would be subject to a defined process. As they continued this perpetual sub-setting, they reduced the number that did not fit into one of their defined classes, so that in a mail dump of 50,000 pieces there would be only a handful of exceptions.

Why did they spend so much time on this process? Because at the volumes they processed, every exception was extremely costly to handle. Any letter that was "different" forced the team to break from its lightning-fast operational rhythm and figure out how to proceed.

Variety Adds Cost and Risk

The remittance handling for Capital One provides stark contrast from what I found at a different national financial services company—one that I won't name here. This company operated a call center in which scores of loan officers granted or denied credit to applicants. What was the process for making these lending decisions? That's a good question.

My team and I were tasked to help the company reduce the costs of the credit reports, court records, and other information sources used in the lending process. As we investigated which products were required, we found that the loan officers were using a wide range of products. The different products were needed because the various loan officers approached their lending judgments in different ways. Some relied almost exclusively on credit scores and salaries; others surveyed employment histories and included traffic court information; others took rent and credit card payments into account.

Here's what this do-it-your-way approach meant: if I called in and requested a loan and talked to George, he might follow his process and conclude I wasn't worth the risk. If I called a different day and spoke with Louise, she would consider different information and grant me the loan.

The bank was spending more than it needed to on information costs—but that was just the beginning of the expense.

The decentralized decision-making increased the time and variation of every application. The bank's representatives had to make judgment calls instead of following strict criteria and processes, and this approach greatly increased the risk. It wasn't simply business risk of making bad loans, but the legal risk of providing uneven lending decisions that were not bolstered by a uniform process. In this case, a lending officer's saying "I do things a bit differently" could have led to the company being sued and possibly even shut down.

WHERE BEING DIFFERENT IS USEFUL

At this point some readers may suspect that the author's version of utopia is a one-size-fits-all, "any color you like as long as it's black" world... a kind of robotic paradise with no variety.[16] Not so! The point of this section is not to argue against variety and difference, but to fully account for the cost and risk that are brought with exceptions.

There are some places where it is helpful—if not necessary—to be different. In fact, some of the most basic and important aspects of an organization are greatly served by being unique. Here are some areas where the right differences can be embraced:

- **A DISTINCTIVE BRAND.** It's not good if the marketplace can't tell you apart from your competitors. When customers know what you stand for and have specific reasons to prefer your products, then your brand is unique in a positive way. *Warning*: If your brand does not extend beyond your products, then competitors with similar offerings may encroach on your brand. (When Quiznos invested in a national advertising campaign with the tagline "Mmm... toasty," it was just as likely to make a viewer's mouth water for a hot sub from a different sandwich store.)

- **A UNIQUE STRATEGY.** If your plan is to do what everyone else in your field is doing—and just do it a little bit better—then you don't really have a strategy. The best strategy should leverage the ways you are different and be a plan for success that your competitors cannot readily copy. A unique strategy can allow you to own your own hill instead of sharing someone else's mountain.

- **A CULTURE THAT IS YOUR OWN.** One of the best paths to success is to fill your team with people who embrace and reflect your brand and strategy. Recruiting all-stars is easier when the culture of an organization is strong enough to attract the right people and make the mismatches easy to identify. (More on culture in the next section.)

- **A DIVERSE TEAM.** Great teams have a clear purpose and a strong culture with shared values, and they are composed of people with different backgrounds and perspectives. One of the best defenses against the negative consequences of believing "we're different" is to involve people from different backgrounds and encourage them to challenge assumptions.

Brand, strategy, culture, and team makeup can all work in concert to generate success and impact. There are wonderful books about these topics, and noteworthy examples of companies that lead their industries by being different in these ways. Yet none of the successful stories are different in haphazard ways; the differences align with the teams and advance their respective missions.

Sorting out the "Good Different" and "Bad Different"

The crafty Expensive Sentence "we're different" deals in partial truths. Our mission must be to recognize and preserve the good different while rooting out the bad different.

When a CEO boasts that "what makes us different is our people," she is not advertising a squadron of misfits and malcontents. Companies go to great lengths to build distinctive cultures that attract the specific kind of talent that drives them to the top of their respective industries. These top performers are not just "good people" in an abstract sense; they are the best people to fit into the company's culture and to execute actions that advance the company's purpose.

Consider how Ritz-Carlton prizes customer service, how Cirque de Soleil attracts artistic creativity, and how Google is a magnet for genius-level innovators. Distinctive team cultures are different in an intentional and positive way. Those differences extend to policies and often separate companies from others in their industry.

Imagine that a well-meaning human resources director proposed the implementation of a new global timecard system for Cirque de Soleil. Or in a cost-cutting measure, a CFO cut in half the fabled discretionary allowance granted to Ritz-Carlton employees to meet customer requests. Or a new COO instructed Google employees to spend less time collaborating so they could get their jobs done more efficiently.

Any of those suggestions might rightly be rejected with the rationale "we can't do that here... we're different." While other companies might wisely save money with those measures, the steps would be absolutely wrong for Ritz, Cirque, and Google. Why are they wrong? Because they would undermine the qualities that led to the competitive differentiation for each of those companies.

These examples highlight the importance of knowing the areas where being different is strategically relevant for your team. Any difference can be instructive, and it should prompt a question: Is your difference genuinely in an area where you are leading the market, or does it reveal a place that you are lagging?

It's also worth asking if your difference is permitted or feasible. In American football, there are teams that emphasize defense, others that feature an offense based on short passes, and others that major on the running game. At the same time, no team is exempt from the rules of the game or the boundaries of the field. These constraints are exactly the same for all teams, and even a team with a very distinctive culture and identity cannot change those parameters without being penalized or disqualified.

Our companies are subject to forces that are beyond our control and that we cannot change. The "rules" may be market fluctuations, seasonality, regulations, innovation, or pressure from new competitors. It doesn't matter how "different" we are—we have no protection from those forces. To succeed, we must account for them and plan accordingly.

DIAGNOSING WHEN "WE'RE DIFFERENT" GOES WRONG

When "different" goes awry, it follows one of two directions. Sometimes an overgrown version of differentiation turns distinctive strengths into arrogance and a denial of competitive threats. At other times, the source of feeling different is the exact opposite of arrogance. Instead of feeling destined to victory, a team feels condemned to the fate of those left behind. These two negative versions of "we're different" don't look anything like each other, so we'll examine them one at a time.

WHEN "WE'RE DIFFERENT" MEANS "WE'RE BETTER"

"We're different" might be just a polite way to boast. The arrogance may be subtle or even subconscious, but the idea that a team or person is above others can lead to poor decisions.

A belief in superiority can take different shapes, some of which may seem benign or even charming. A homeowner who resists buying insurance because he can't imagine an accident may not be an arrogant person, but at some level he is exempting himself from the regular events of life. Blissful newlyweds may tell each other "those couples argue, but that will never happen to us." Or—with sometimes tragic results—the parent in denial might say "my son would never take drugs" and overlook telling signals or fail to take precautions.

Business history holds many examples of superiority that could never be displaced—until it was. Sometimes these beliefs of "we're different" or "that could never happen to us" were held at a national level. In the 1960s, with World War II in vivid memory, it was widely believed that U.S. car buyers would never prefer Japanese cars over Detroit's production. Decades later, analysts around the world stated that Korea could never successfully challenge high-quality Japanese cars. In both cases, events ultimately proved the experts wrong, and the consequences changed national economies and millions of lives.

Your team might hold beliefs rooted in the superiority of your company, products, or reputation. Perhaps it's unthinkable that a certain marquis customer would ever leave you. You may believe that a competitor could never surpass your technology or product design.

There is a place for a healthy ego and self-confidence in business. After all, if you don't believe you have a better solution, you're not likely ever to get your product to the marketplace. At the same time, the targets of excellence are constantly moving. Superiority breeds complacency. If "we're different" statements reveal a belief that your company is inherently better than another, it may lead to the opposite result.

Hearing the Different Drummer

In American culture, there's a romance to being unique, blazing a new trail, and even rebelling. After all, our country began by (figuratively) moving out of our parents' house in England and then telling them to mind their own business. Our founding documents affirm the rights of the individual. American literature celebrates the trailblazer, perhaps most lyrically by Henry David Thoreau:

> If a man does not keep pace with his companions, perhaps it is because he hears a different drummer. Let him step to the music which he hears, however measured or far away.[17]

Many fabled American business heroes are those who heard a different drummer. Thomas Edison, Henry Ford, and Steve Jobs were revolutionary leaders who saw themselves as different, took bold actions, and created innovations that have changed literally billions of lives for the better.

It is true that new enterprises often spring directly from one person's passion to do things differently and better. Somehow creative individualism seems to live on the same street as arrogance. We need to be careful to nurture one while not over-feeding the other.

Also, we should use caution when adopting a celebrated, genius-level individualist like those mentioned above as a role model. There is no guarantee of repeating such success without the same level of talent, the right historical timing, and probably a large measure of luck. It's also worth noting that some luminaries paid great personal costs and inflicted pain on those around them as they pursued their dreams.

When "We're Different" Means "We're Worse"

If arrogance can cause problems, believing that you're not as good as someone else can be just as troublesome. (And it will probably be a rather dreary experience.) The minor variation of the Expensive Sentence "we're different" is the idea that the team is inferior to others or constrained so that it cannot do what others can. This notion emerges in statements that sound resigned, defeated, or fatalistic: "we're different, so we can't...." They bring to mind the story of the three caterpillars:

> *Three caterpillars were crawling through the dirt one day when they spotted a stunning black and yellow butterfly, beautifully dancing in the air.*
>
> *The first caterpillar jabbed: "Look at that showoff. Flitting around up there like he's Mr. Big."*
>
> *The second one sighed. "Wow. Some days I wish I could fly."*
>
> *The third caterpillar took a long look at the butterfly. Then he spoke slowly, and with determination: "I remember that guy. He used to be one of us. If he can do it, I can do it."*

Does the third caterpillar with the "can-do" attitude embody the spirit of your team? Or are you surrounded by caterpillars like the first two? A short checklist of questions can identify whether your team may see itself as different in a negative way:

- Can you keep up with your competitors?
- Are you able to attract top talent in your industry?
- Can you keep your customers delighted by improving your offering?

If the answer to any of those questions is negative, then "we're different" might be language that covers cynicism, defeatism, or pessimism. These attitudes need to be contained and converted because few things are more destructive than unbridled negativity. Sour people can destroy families, churches, companies, schools, clubs, and any other group of people.

Before you blame the "caterpillars," though, it's worth exploring where their attitudes came from. The malaise may indicate a larger problem, and it may be a byproduct of company leadership.

THE ROOT OF DEFEATISM

Diagnosing why your team believes it can't do things that others can will help you understand how serious the beliefs are and plan a corrective course of action. Before you mandate happy-face pins or adopt the pirate captain's approach that "beatings will continue until morale improves," consider that the lethargy of your organization may be a direct result of how it was trained. Let's identify some of the most common sources of defeated thinking.

Negative People at the Top

People tend to hire in their own image. This principle may apply to gender, ethnicity, and educational background, but it also extends to outlook and attitude. Sour managers don't attract optimistic world-beaters. If your management team includes a grumpy naysayer, his worldview is likely to spread at least through his department. As the old saying goes, "the fish rots from the head." Management is the first place to look when evaluating the mood of the team.

Recent Trauma

Teams go through tough seasons. If your group recently experienced layoffs, or has just retrenched and cut salaries, or if a major initiative flopped publicly, the team may feel that loss and fear a repeat of some sort. Success breeds more success, and setbacks likewise carry the danger of replicating themselves.

Lack of Follow-Through by Leadership

Perfect communication is a unicorn; it doesn't exist on any team. At times the words of leadership do not appear to align with the actions of leadership. The team may perceive a high-level disconnect if, for example, a company claims to be a leader in innovation, but few dollars are spent on research and development. Or a specific promise might be orphaned: maybe the CEO stated at a company meeting that a stock option program would be introduced in the third quarter, and when the quarter ended, nothing happened.

When actions do not match words—even in perception—there is a consequence. When this pattern repeats in leadership, those on the team face a practical decision: do they believe again (and subject themselves to disappointment) or do they hear those words with a measure of skepticism? The natural result of disappointment is cynicism, and the natural result of cynicism is disengagement.

Burned by Past Experiences

Consider a sales VP who comes back from a conference with a new book and a load of enthusiasm. "I just learned all about the New Wave plan for selling better. This is going to make a huge difference for us!" The team hires consultants, learns a new vocabulary, re-works their funnel structure, sets new quotas, and goes hard after the new approach.

Eighteen months later, sales are disappointing; the numbers are roughly the same as they were before the team started the new program.

The fact that the effort did not succeed does not necessarily mean that pursuing it was wrong. But a salesperson on the team might bring less gusto into the next new system, particularly if they don't see leaders exert a genuine effort to learn from the defeat and take measures to ensure that future efforts will be more successful.

Any remedy can be over-prescribed or wrongly applied. Sometimes the scars and memories of those past mistakes lead to the objections of being different. If you hear "we've tried that before, it never works," it is worth unpacking that organizational weariness to explore its origin. If the pessimism is not addressed, it may well become a self-fulfilling prophecy with the next new program.

Defining Difference with the Right Focus

As a leader on your team, how do you promote the right level of differentiation, but eschew the dangerous "we're different" type of thinking?

Max Depree, the former CEO of furniture maker Herman Miller and the author of *Leadership Is an Art*, asserted that "the first responsibility of a leader is to define reality." It's worth noting a similar quote attributed to Napoleon Bonaparte: "The leader's role is to define reality, then give hope."

Sometimes the best way for a leader to define reality is by changing focus. That may mean drawing the team's attention from the trees to the forest, or at least from one tree to a different tree. When you're defining how a team is different, it is especially important to have an external focus—one that does not look inward to the team but instead emphasizes the team's relationship with the outside world. Specifically, a team can consider the customer, their results, and their actions.

- **FOCUS ON THE CUSTOMER** — An outward-focused team will not drown in self-reflection or make excuses. If an organization puts solving the customers' problems above all else—including even their own capability and limitations—it is more likely to find the right path forward.

- **FOCUS ON RESULTS** — Teams that feel defeated often bemoan their circumstances or lack of resources. A shift in focus from resources to results may help a team reconnect with its purpose. With determined resolve to achieve results, differences either become advantages in reaching the goal or barriers that must be overcome.

- **FOCUS ON ACTION** — "We're different" thinking can start with legitimate differences, but then lead to self-pity, justification, resignation, and inaction. Positive differences lead to useful actions. If you must discuss the past and the present, limit the time spent on those subjects and then pivot to positive next steps.

WISE REPLIES TO "WE'RE DIFFERENT"

. . . .

We have reviewed the costs and the concepts, and now it's time to get practical. In the remainder of this chapter we will review sample language, conversation topics, and exercises that you can apply with your team to avoid the Special myth that you are different.

RESPONDING DIRECTLY TO EXPENSIVE SENTENCES

If perceived differences on your team are leading to dangerous defeatism or arrogance, you can change the conversation. Try adapting one of the scripts below:

" *Does that difference matter to our* CEO? *Does it matter to the customer?"*

" *Yes, we are different. Let's write down the top three ways in which we are different. Do you think we* SHOULD *be different in these ways? Why? Why not?"*

" *Do you think our number-one competitor would be different in the same way? Is it possible we could fall behind if we don't change?"*

" *It's OK if we're different, but if this is the right thing to do, nothing should keep us from doing it."*

" *The way I see it is: We have to deal with customers. We have to deal with employees. We have to think about cost. So in those most important areas, I don't think we are really different. Are we?"*

GROUP CONVERSATION TOPICS

If the themes of being special or different repeatedly show up in your team conversations, it may be helpful to set aside some time to discuss several general topics:

- Are we better than other companies? Why? How?

- Are we expecting others (employees, vendors, customers) to behave differently than we've seen in the past?

- Are we seeing other people as they are, or as we want to see them?

- Do we think there are things we cannot do?

EXERCISES TO EVALUATE DIFFERENCES

The actions and exercises below can help you manage being different on your team. There are more resources and exercises on *www.ExpensiveSentences.com*.

EXERCISE: DRIVE OUT EXCEPTIONS

If you suspect that your operations are not as efficient as they could be or that your team might be spending too much time on exception-handling, take steps to streamline operations.

Automation is not just for factories. Any group that handles some sort of task repeatedly has the opportunity to improve the speed and quality of operations by instituting processes, procedures, and standardization. This may not be intuitive to your team, but you can lead them through a process of "perpetual sub-setting" to reduce exceptions.

1. Ask team members to log their time and activities for a week (that is, at the end of each day write down how they spent their time that day)

2. The next week, meet again and review that results together. How much time is spent on routine activities that could possibly be improved or automated?

3. Within the time spent on routine activities, how much time is spent handling exceptions?

4. Discuss the specific exceptions:

    a. Do any groups emerge among the exceptions?

    b. Could an additional process be added so that some of the exceptions were handled in a standardized way?

    c. Would it be better to handle most of the exceptions together, or have one person focusing on the exceptions?

The goal is to engage your team in reducing exceptions. It may be useful to meet on an ongoing basis. Don't forget to celebrate the wins: any process that is automated, routinized, documented, or otherwise improved will lower cost and risk.

EXERCISE: EXTERNAL/INTERNAL SURVEY... AND FOLLOW UP

Company management may have a well-defined brand strategy, but that doesn't necessarily mean that the strategy is working in the marketplace or even within the company. To learn the reality of how you are perceived, you can ask. A short survey using a free web survey tool can be a quick and effective way to gain information about how your efforts at differentiation are actually working.

As with any survey or marketing research, the goal is to learn something that is actionable, not simply interesting. To that end, it is best to reverse-engineer the questions you will ask. Start by brainstorming a list of potential outcomes from the survey. The actions might range from small tweaks (improve communications internally, start a new culture training class, add a quarterly client check-in call) to major changes (re-direct company strategy, re-work vision statement, hire consultant to transform culture, change executive responsibilities, etc.). If you cannot reasonably see yourself making some meaningful changes after the survey, then there is no reason to gather the information.

Internal Survey

Within your company, you may want to ask a few open-ended questions, such as:

- How is working for this company different from other places you have worked?

- Where are we different in positive ways?

- How are we different in negative ways?

- Does it seem like there are things we should be able to do, but don't or can't?

If you want unfiltered truth, consider making the survey anonymous. Remember that you will be judged by how you respond to the findings: if you are going to ask your team for input, be ready to receive it, believe it, and take action based on what you learn.

External Survey

Your customers, prospects, former customers, and maybe even your competitors are good sources for how you are seen in the marketplace. Some simple branding questions can be helpful:

- How would you describe our brand in a few words?
- How different is our company from others that do similar functions?
- Are we different in ways that enhance our service to you?
- Are we different in ways that may diminish our service to you?

The same guideline applies about only asking for data that will lead to action, and about responding to all information you receive. In the case of participants that are not your customers, you can respond simply by sending a thank you note and sharing one or two items that you learned from the survey. Your customers would probably appreciate an acknowledgment that their time spent responding to the survey will improve their service.

CHAPTER 5

"WE TRUST THEM"

"They're not just vendors, they're partners."

"We don't need to know all the details;
we trust them."

"Let's not micromanage; they are professionals."

"We can always count on her."

We wouldn't get far without trust.

Every day we trust alarm clocks to wake us at the right time. We trust bus drivers to take our children to school, and teachers to care for them. We trust thousands of people whom we have never met to follow traffic laws and keep their automobiles under control. We trust elevators and escalators and countless other machines. We trust those who package, transport, and prepare food. We trust merchants, large and small, reputable and unknown, to take our financial information and not abuse it.

When you think it through, our level of trust in the people, systems, and structures around us is remarkable. Even the more cynical among us operate on a foundation of widespread trust.

THE COST OF BROKEN TRUST

Given our dependence on trust, it's no surprise that we tend to trust the people we spend time with and the companies we work with. At the same time, we all encounter failures of trust with some regularity:

- We trust a meeting organizer to invite the right people to an event, but he omits one of the key participants. Because of that oversight, the time is less productive and the overlooked person may be offended.

- We trust that a vendor is billing us correctly, but find that the agreed-upon discounts have not been applied so we are spending more than we should be.

- We trust a colleague to review our work and provide input during the drafting process, but she instead criticizes the finished product in a public way, causing embarrassment.

- We trust that a teammate will complete a task by an agreed-upon deadline, but the work is not done in time. The delay affects the project's schedule and adds additional cost and wasted time.

- We trust a friend to bring a prepared dish to a social event, but he forgets to. The meal is incomplete, and the event does not meet our hopes.

None of these examples rise to the level of betrayal, and some may amount to little more than a nuisance. Yet they all add cost to our lives in various ways: added financial cost, wasted time, loss of opportunities, diminished reputation, lower quality, less enjoyment, added stress and worry, etc.

When we tally up the various costs of these "minor" violations of trust, we see that they may have a greater impact than we realize. Of course, when breakdowns in trust rise above the mundane level to ethical failure, the fallout can destroy careers and relationships.

TRUST BETRAYED

Years ago, I received a phone call from the CEO of a thirty-person company. He was both a client and a friend, and as soon as I heard his voice, I knew that something was wrong. From his tone, I feared that he had just learned of tragic health news or a death in the family.

"Steven, are you OK?" I asked.

"Not really."

"Is someone hurt?" I asked. He assured me that no one was in physical peril and then proceeded to tell me the story. The owner of the company had been reviewing credit card statements and saw some unexplained charges. After weeks of thorough, painstaking review, Steven and the company owner found clear evidence that the accounting clerk—who had worked for the company for more than ten years—had been stealing money from the company.

The pain and consequences from this fraud went in many directions. Immediately the company invested in upgraded physical and electronic security to prevent additional thefts. The company had to pay for a comprehensive audit to determine the full amount of the embezzlement. They had to make sure that no one else was involved in the fraud, and they needed new policies and procedures for all of their financial operations.

Beyond these financial costs was the toll on morale and relationships. Many difficult conversations ensued: first with attorneys and management, then with the clerk, and finally with everyone at the company. As a small company, it was close-knit and many described it as a family. Many on the team felt betrayed.

Because he knew the accounting clerk well, Steven felt partially responsible for the failure. He asked himself if he should have seen this coming or should have taken more precautions to prevent a situation where financial abuse was even possible. "I wonder if I'll ever trust anyone on my team again," he told me.

My friend was fortunate that this experience with fraud wasn't even more damaging. The financial loss was limited to five figures, and the deceit limited to one employee. Things would have been far worse if other employees had been involved or if the clerk had taken actions that affected any of the company's clients. In the aftermath of the incident, Steven imagined having to call his customers and explain that someone on his team had been stealing from them.

BROKEN TRUST

We all know the pain and cost of broken trust personally, at least at some level. We can see failures of trust in the lives of our friends, in history, and in current events. Is there anything we can do to lessen those consequences in our own lives? Can we reduce our reliance on trust, and still maintain a positive outlook and good relationships?

Fortunately, the answer to both of those questions is yes. But we may have to re-evaluate the way we think about trust, and even how we define the word.

While trustworthiness seems like a moral virtue, we'll see that many failures of trust have absolutely nothing to do with ethics. We'll unpack the different dimensions of trust, and we'll also see why in some cases the best way to increase trust in the long-term is to trust less in the near-term.

CHANGING HOW WE THINK ABOUT TRUST

I am a trusting person by nature. It's not just that I am inclined to trust others; I deeply want to trust others. I want to believe that others will behave honorably and honestly.

Alas, experience has taught me that people cannot always be trusted. That's life, as Sinatra sang, and "as funny as it seems, some people get their kicks stepping on a dream." So I have learned to be realistic about human nature. Beyond that, I have learned that trust involves much more than finding honest people with good intentions.

TRUST IS MULTI-DIMENSIONAL

In his book *The Speed of Trust,* Steven M. Covey breaks trust into two classes: character and competence. This is a useful distinction because not every breakdown in trust is related to moral or character issues.

Consider the anecdote about the accounting clerk. Imagine that instead of the fraud described, the CEO had discovered that the clerk had honestly but incompetently gotten the company books into a huge mess. That would still be a problem, but it would not carry even a fraction of the betrayal and regret associated with embezzlement. On the other hand, imagine that the meeting organizer in the earlier example had excluded the key person from your event not as an oversight, but as a way to undermine your career. The saboteur's nefarious intent would make his actions ten times worse.

These what-ifs show the importance of separating character and competence. Without this distinction, trust becomes overly loaded with ethical baggage so that any question of trust is a challenge to someone's decency or moral virtue. This sensitivity means that we are less likely to talk about trust and leads us to assume too much.

TRUST IS NOT ALL-OR-NOTHING

We are prone to use a broad brush when speaking about trust. We say things like "he's in a position of trust" or "I trust her implicitly" or "I would trust you with my life." On the negative side, we proclaim that we'll "never trust them again" or "I wouldn't trust him farther than I can throw him" or "you can't trust that guy."

These phrases do not serve us well. They imply that trust is monolithic and binary: someone either deserves every kind of trust all of the time or is never worthy of any kind of trust. That might be how we feel, particularly as we endure painful consequences of broken trust. But in reality there is more nuance to trust.

We naturally apply circumstances to trust when we award it to others. For example, I might trust the chef at the local diner to make a beautiful Greek salad, but I wouldn't trust him to watch my toddler for an afternoon. I may trust my father with my finances and even my life, but not trust him to pick out a necktie that matches his shirt. My pastor might be trusted to dispense reliable wisdom about raising children, but I wouldn't let him try to remove my appendix. (You get the idea.)

Context matters. Trust must be qualified: whom do we trust to do what, in which situations, and how far does that trust extend? Declarations that someone either can't be trusted or should always be trusted are false absolutes that may become Expensive Sentences. In fact, nearly every relationship is characterized by both trust and lack of trust in different areas.

TRUST TRANSFERS AND EXPANDS

Years ago, a partner and I were working together on a tech startup. I led the fundraising piece, and he led the operations. We outsourced the product development to a vendor, who was working on a prototype. As the fundraiser, I was eager to show the prototype to potential investors. Since my partner was responsible for the development, I asked him if we could check in with the developer to make sure that we would be ready to demonstrate the product by the scheduled date. My partner replied, "Let the man do his work. He'll get it done by the deadline." I was comforted by my partner's trust in the developer.

By the time the deadline came, I had lined up several investor meetings for the following weeks. But the prototype wasn't ready, so there was nothing to show the investors. Finally our developer finished the prototype… months after the deadline. The delay was agonizing, and it probably cost us opportunities to secure investment dollars.

I was disgusted. I wished I had pushed harder and demanded that we check in with the developer. It might not have sped the process, but at least I would have had a more realistic delivery date and then presented that to investors. But I didn't insist upon the check-in because I wanted to trust my partner, and I wanted to believe that we could trust our vendor.

Because my partner had too much trust in his vendor, it weakened my trust in him. That may be unfair, but I depended on him for my own reputation. I had led potential investors to believe that I could show them the demonstration after the original deadline. The delay most certainly weakened their trust in me. This loss of credibility was devastating for a startup because trust was the only real currency we had—our entire business proposition was built on assumptions that we could deliver. It was a chain of trust:

POTENTIAL INVESTORS ▶ ME ▶ MY PARTNER ▶ THE DEVELOPER

Of course, the investors trust in me wasn't based entirely on the developer's output; there were other factors. But when the developer failed to come through on his part, the trust breakdown cascaded from him to my partner, from my partner to me, and from me to the investors. It reminded me of an old proverb:

> For want of a nail the shoe was lost; for want of a shoe the horse was lost; for want of a horse the rider was lost.[18]

The way that trust is borrowed, transferred, and leveraged makes it still more critical to place trust in the right places. But fear not: when we remember that trust is not always connected to character, and that trust is always relative to context, it makes trust more manageable.

MANAGING TRUST

There is no reason that we can't improve our skills in trust management, just as we can improve our skills in time management or money management. Trust is just as important as those other resources, and too critical to leave to assumptions and good intentions. We can analyze trust and be savvy about how and when we rely upon it as we are working with others.

I will assume that you conduct business with those who meet your ethical standards. But after clearing that bar of basic decency, you will still have questions about trust:

- *What* would you trust them to do?

- Do you trust them to do it *well*?

- *In what circumstances* do you trust them?

- Do you trust them to do it in a *timely* manner?

Sometimes it is better to ask questions in the negative: What do you NOT trust them to do? Or, where would you be wise to withhold trust, at least for now?

After my episode with the startup and the software developer, it occurred to me that a measure of skepticism and withheld trust early on can sometimes save a great deal of broken trust later.

IN DEFENSE OF MICROMANAGING

It's better to be called a "micromanager" than a "bigot," but you probably won't put either on your business card. Micromanaging seems to be a universally disliked practice. It makes sense that few people would ask to be micromanaged, because it may imply a lack of confidence. But we can also concede that there are degrees of oversight, and what one person believes is micromanagement could be viewed by someone else as helpful support or guidance.

Since we don't have absolute trust even in the people closest to us, why would we fully trust someone else to get a particular job done the right way? Or, to take more personal ownership, why would we trust ourselves to communicate perfectly and equip someone to succeed on the first try, without checking in to make sure things are going in the right direction?

It's important to examine the stigma against micromanaging because otherwise we may shun it in a way that is unfair to ourselves and those who work for us. Ronald Reagan is often quoted for his maxim "trust, but verify" related to Cold War weapons treaties. This saying is a helpful reminder that trust and verification are not mutually exclusive.

WE DON'T TRUST OURSELVES COMPLETELY

Let's consider how much we trust ourselves, and how we manage ourselves. For example, we may trust ourselves to choose the right career and the right spouse, but not trust ourselves to replace a ceiling lamp correctly or remember the name of someone we meet for the first time at a networking event.

In those areas where we don't trust ourselves, we often employ tools or supports to lessen the burden on trust. We might hire an electrician or handyman to fix the lamp, and we might write down the name of someone or ask for their business card when we first meet them.

If our goal is to lose weight and eat healthier—and if we're serious about succeeding—we'll stock up on healthy food and get the cookies and potato chips out of the house. Why do we move the junk food? Because at some level we don't trust ourselves to eat the right things. In my case, I might say, "I trust myself to make good decisions and be healthy." But at the same time, I might add, "After a long day of work and avoiding junk food, I don't trust myself after 9:00 to eat a healthy snack. Because I want to stay with my diet, I am going to remove this temptation so I am more likely to succeed." (Let's hope I don't sound so robotic when I talk to myself… but you can't fault the logic.)

Limited self-trust could be seen as weak willpower or a lack of self-control. At a principled level, we might like to think that we have the discipline and strength to follow our eating plan, no matter which foods might drift across our culinary transom. But from a practical point of view—alas—we are more likely to have success when we banish the sweet, salty, and starchy treats.

The pragmatic approach can help us in working with others. If it's worth clearing our own path of temptations and potential pitfalls, wouldn't we be kind to do the same for someone else?

SETTING PEOPLE UP FOR SUCCESS

When managing trust in professional relationships, the goal is similar to that of the dieter: not to test willpower, but to increase the likelihood of good decisions and actions. We can preserve trust by having fewer areas in which it is exercised. In the workplace there are innumerable ways to set people up for success and to reduce the extent to which trust is relied upon. Here is a partial list:

- Documenting processes

- Employing checklists

- Having multiple draft iterations of documents

- Breaking up projects into reviewable milestones

- Reporting progress frequently, or on a pre-set schedule

- Using redundant communication (that is, repeating yourself… get it?)

- Requiring review signatures or approval at multiple levels

While process enthusiasts (like the author) could put these bullet points to music, some of you are feeling a physical revulsion to an onslaught of tactics that seem bureaucratic and invasive. You may be thinking: *Can't I just hire great people and let them handle these details?* Sure, it's quite possible that you can. Plus, I'm not saying that you would or should implement all of the safeguards above.

But what's the harm of better definition? What would it cost to put any two things on the list into practice? Here's an equally important question: what's the price of failure or misunderstanding?

The accounting clerk in our prior story did something wrong, and endured the consequences of those actions. Here's what I wonder about my friend's company: if there had been better controls and greater visibility in place before the incident, might that have prevented this accounting clerk from taking the wrong steps? Or to put it another way, would it have served the clerk to have been trusted less, and might that even have prevented a life-altering personal tragedy?

When we hire a vendor or an employee, we like to think we're getting the best. But the truth is, we don't always get employees and vendors at their best, and sometimes we get them at their worst. This fact can inform the way we plan and the way we treat those around us. We want to plan for maximum success, not maximum reliance on trust.

It is not disrespectful or untrusting to put banisters on a stairway. The added measures toward trust that we install in our working patterns can perform a similar function of helping people support themselves or know where the boundaries are.

TRUSTING BUSINESS "PARTNERS"

When a salesperson says "We're not just vendors, we're *partners*" it can set the stage for excessive trust. The implication is that the self-pro-claimed partners—unlike some companies that are simply looking for a paycheck—are good guys who value their clients' success as much as their own.

My cynical take on the difference between a vendor and a partner is that a partner has permission to charge 10 percent more. Okay, that's flippant, and maybe you're one of the people who uses the language of partnership with your customers and lives up to that spirit. But for some vendors, calling themselves partners doesn't amount to more substance than when a laundry detergent sports a "New and Improved!" sticker.

Literal partnerships are financial arrangements in which the partners share costs and potential rewards. It's easier to trust a true partner because he has money on the line just like I do, and by "trusting" him I am actually just believing that he will act in his own self-interest.

As a guiding principle that rarely fails, we can trust individuals and organizations to act in their own interests. When we find those whose interests are harmonious with our own, we have the potential for a working relationship that is beneficial to everyone. Then we can review the dimensions that will influence whether, how much, and in what ways to trust.

ASSESSING TRUST: FOUR ESSENTIAL CHECKPOINTS

Earlier I referenced Steven Covey's model delineating trust into character and competency aspects. In a professional relationship, where our goal is to avoid the expense of too much or misplaced trust, we can add two more "C's" so that our trust is defined by four components:

1. Character

2. Competence

3. Capacity

4. Communication

These building blocks of trust are sequential; there is no reason to add the second one until you are confident of the first, and so on. It's notable that capacity and communication are not explicitly related to either character or competence. Yet their function is just as important. When trust breaks down and things go wrong, the problem often stems from the logistics of a working relationship.

Trust in Character

Basic honesty is not a high bar, but integrity can extend to wider issues. Are the person's words clear and not misleading? Do people follow through on things when they say they will? Do they keep appointments? Failures in these areas can have a corrosive effect on relationships. (I've heard stories in which someone says in retrospect, "I knew I couldn't trust him when he cancelled that appointment… I should have backed out then.")

My experience suggests that failures of follow-through, punctuality, and organization can sometimes indicate substantive issues, and sometimes do not. But if one of those housekeeping items matters to you, let it matter to you. Do not ignore your intuition. At a minimum, you can raise a question with the person and see how they respond: "I noticed that we had to reschedule our meeting twice, and at our organization it really is important to keep our appointments. Does that make sense, and can you adjust to that?"

Trust in Competence

With someone you can trust ethically, the next obvious question is about their competence or ability. Can they get the job done? The first place to start is with basic questions:

- Do they understand the job requirements?

- Do they understand the intended results of the job?

- Have they done it before?

- Have they done it for someone in a situation similar to yours?

As the job complexity increases, specific knowledge and experience may become less important than professionalism and ability to learn. For example, if your industry is highly regulated and you are hiring a general counsel, it is important not simply that the person knows the current law but also that they demonstrate a commitment to keeping up with new legislation.

TRUST IN CAPACITY: PRIORITY AND AVAILABILITY

Character and competence are essential, but many relationships that clear these hurdles still end up in frustration and disappointment. Often that occurs because of a problem in capacity. If someone I trust is capable of doing the job I need, I need to ask if she is going to do it in a timeframe and manner that are acceptable to me.

Exploring How a Vendor Will Deliver

When you're hiring a vendor, a clear contract with defined deliverables can minimize assumptions. If everyone knows what the finished job looks like, there is less room for misunderstanding. But when the product of the relationship is less tangible, more discussion is needed and there are more questions to ask:

- Does the vendor have the necessary resources?

- Will their best people be on the team?

- Who will be leading the engagement?

- What should you expect in terms of response time?

- How will you communicate? (Email, text, phone, in-person?)

- Will they be on-site, and if so, how many hours a week?

This may seem like micromanaging. (And despite the brilliant earlier section, you might still resist micromanaging.) It may feel awkward or even insulting to talk through the operational details. But asking the extra questions can help you avoid disappointing surprises:

- "Bill was the guy who walked us through the sales process and learned everything about our requirements, but then after we signed the deal, he seemed to disappear."

- "Our prior vendor would always get back to me the same day, but with the new company, we seem to be less of a priority. I guess they are busy with their bigger customers."

- "They switched our account lead to a new hire. She was very nice, but she didn't have the experience and I think that cost us."

The good news is that these "little things" can often be corrected and trust can be restored. But it's far better to prevent these disappointments altogether by explicitly discussing the details before trust declines.

TRUST IN COMMUNICATION

Character, competence, and capability form a solid foundation of trust for a working relationship. Yet trust can still break down in the daily routine, and one of the most common trouble spots is communication.

Communication is an area in which less trust would usually be a good thing. If the other party does not clearly understand our situation, our goals, or our priorities, they are far less likely to act efficiently on our behalf. It's better to risk over-communicating—or even to be perceived as a pest—than to have to say one of these easily avoidable regrets:

- "I thought everyone knew our top priority, but I should have said it out loud."

- "I didn't want to offend him by repeating myself. I wish I had."

It is amazing how many thorny problems can be cleaned up with one conversation.

Years ago I ran operations for a startup company that outsourced bill management for large companies. Our first two customer installations went well, but the third one was bumpy. In fact, the customer was so unhappy after three months that they threatened to fire us. I visited the client to see if there might be some ways we could add more value and save the relationship.

What I found was illuminating… and alarming. Instead of using our automated system, the client was printing out our reports and then retyping them into their old system. No wonder they complained that we weren't saving them any money—they probably had to work harder than before to make these dual systems work together. We had assumed that they would use our system as we intended. It was obvious to us, but not so to them.

Knowing when and how to trust our customers relates to the theme of expertise. Because you are more of an expert on your product than your clients are, it is your responsibility to ensure that they can get the full value that you deliver. Are you ensuring impact and results with your clients, or are you trusting that they are getting the most from your relationship?

WISE **R**EPLIES TO **"W**E TRUST THEM**"**

. . . .

You don't have to be a cynic to question whether your team may be trusting too much. In fact, you can decrease cynicism by reducing the risk of getting burned by over-trusting.

RESPONDING DIRECTLY TO EXPENSIVE SENTENCES

When you or a teammate drops an Expensive Sentence that implies a reliance on trust, there is an opportunity to improve the conversation. Try responding along one of the following lines:

> **❝** *I absolutely trust Chuck's character. I'd trust him with my life. But I know he has a lot going on right now, and I'm not sure if we have communicated to him just how urgent our situation is. So let's ask him to give us weekly updates on his progress, at least until we hit the next milestone."*

> **❝** *That vendor has a great reputation, and I'm sure they are trustworthy. But I want to call the reference checks anyway. I'm not sure their other clients have used them the way we intend to."*

> **❝** *Yes, we trust them, but I trust them most to do what is in their own interests."*

> **❝** *Karen, I trust you on this, but I've learned not to trust myself to always communicate the most important things. So if you don't mind, I'd like to review the account and our plan for the meeting."*

❝ *We trust you and I'm sure the stories you have shared are accurate. We still want to see the data you referred to; it just always helps me to see numbers in black and white."*

GROUP CONVERSATION TOPICS

Questioning trust may be considered taboo on your team; you can remedy that with an intentional discussion about how and when you are relying on trust. The following questions are a starting point:

- Where have we seen a breakdown in trust with vendors, donors, employees, or customers in the last two years? Is there anything we could have done differently to have placed less of a burden on trust?

- Where is our team highly dependent on trust? Are there things we could do to reduce our dependence?

- What are our five most important vendor relationships? In these, where do we rely on trust?

- Where is our communication crystal-clear? Where are we leaving things to chance?

- Do our customers consistently get the most value from our products and services? Are we trusting customers to behave a certain way?

EXERCISE: BENCHMARK TO TRUST AND VERIFY

If you are concerned that you may be trusting a single vendor excessively, a few benchmarking discussions with other potential providers can be highly educational. Talking to possible alternatives can give you a reference point for the fees you are paying; it also helps as a sanity check to make sure you are not missing developments in the market. (Remember: every vendor and consultant has blind spots.)

Market benchmarking does not mean you are being unfaithful to your current provider. It is your prerogative as a buyer, and may in fact be your obligation as a steward of company funds. Start by identifying a few potential vendors that might be worth talking to. (If you don't know them already, a short web search will provide your list.) Then simply call one up and ask if you can talk. Here is a template for that conversation:

> *We have another provider that we're generally satisfied with. I don't want to take much of your time, because from my current point of view we're not likely to change, but we don't know what we don't know. I wonder if you might be up for a 45-minute conversation where we can tell you about our situation and let you ask us some questions. If we do get more serious about a change at some point in the future, of course we'll keep you in mind.*

The expertise of the modern sales force is a gold mine that is often overlooked. If you take on this exercise with an open mind, you may be surprised how much you learn.

CHAPTER 6

"THAT'S THE WAY WE'VE ALWAYS DONE IT"

"This is what they taught me to do."

"That's just how we do things here."

"Everybody does it."

"That's the [Army/Navy/Exxon/ (your company name)] way."

YEARS AGO I LED A PROJECT TO HELP A CLIENT MANAGE ITS PHONE BILLS. Our company had developed a top-notch software system to help large organizations automate their invoice processing. The solution included a workflow feature that allowed a user to approve a bill and then have it automatically sent to another approver (at the time, this was rather advanced). In fact, our software supported three levels of approval, which was sufficient to serve the twenty-five clients we had at the time.

This particular client was a bureau of the federal government, and it requested several customizations to support its business processes. Among those changes, the client asked for more levels of approval. How many more levels of approval did they need, you ask? Six more, for a grand total of nine. (Sadly, I had a low awareness of Expensive Sentences at the time; this engagement was a cocktail of "We're different" and "The customer is always right" with a few others thrown in for good measure.) After some deliberation, we decided to customize our software to allow for the bureau's many approvals.

It wasn't until rather late in the engagement that I asked what should have been one of my first questions: what are some reasons that invoices are NOT approved? The bureau employee whom I first asked appeared stumped, and then sheepishly admitted that he had never rejected an invoice; that is, he approved every bill he had ever seen. Then we asked someone else and got the same reply. In fact, we learned that throughout this department, no one ever disapproved bills; they always progressed from the start of the process through nine affirmative approvals and then to payment.

This head-scratching realization prompted the question: "why again are we doing this?" While our system made the nine-level approval more efficient, it served absolutely no practical purpose... because the bills were *always* approved. In customizing our system, it was as if we were replacing a stairway that led nowhere with an escalator.

Why did this bureau go through the process of nine approvals when no one on the team could remember any bill being rejected? Because that was the way they had always done it.

Habits and Coasting

Habits can be good, and inertia isn't always bad. In the same way that automation and processes (as discussed in CHAPTER 2) can lower the cost of operations, habits can allow us to make progress on routine tasks—such as folding clothes or brushing our teeth—while preserving our mental energy for matters that require active thought.

When our days seem to be driven more by habit and routine than by directed purpose, we sometimes say that we are "in a rut." This expression dates back to dirt roads and horse-drawn wagons with narrow, wooden wheels. When it rained, the dirt roads became mud, and wagon wheels would leave deep crevasses behind them. Those crevasses, once dried, became ruts. Afterward, the ruts had the effect of keeping the wagon wheels in the middle of the road.

So a rut was not necessarily a bad thing; in fact, it could help you get to your destination with less friction and effort. There was one critically important qualifier: the rut had to be pointing in the right direction. Otherwise, it would take you somewhere you didn't want to go.

We can bring this vehicular metaphor into modern times. There are moments when we can release the acceleration pedal on our car and coast forward, using momentum to continue in the right direction. But if we let go of the steering wheel and close our eyes, we're not just coasting. We're now drifting, and we may not like where we end up.

We all rely on process and routine as well as habit and precedent. Doing things by default isn't necessarily bad. But drifting can be lethal in an automobile, and it's not advisable for how we live our lives or lead our teams.

THE COSTS OF DRIFTING

If our actions don't efficiently advance our goals—and might in fact counteract our goals—then we incur the obvious costs of wasted time, wasted money, and missed opportunity. These are the most visible costs of doing things because "that's the way we've always done it."

WASTED MONEY

If you know someone who loves to shop the sales, then you may have observed why "It's on sale" is an Expensive Sentence. Paying less for a planned purchase can save us money, and there's nothing wrong with that. But most of us are not always disciplined with our buying practices. A head-turning 40 percent off sale or buy-one-get-one-free offer can prompt us to reach for our credit cards, even if the product is not on our shopping list. "It was such a good deal I couldn't pass it up" is a phrase that has filled many closets with twice-worn sweaters and redundant bathrobes; it is also the retail equivalent of "that's the way we've always done it" as a statement that attempts to justify action without any connection to purpose.

If you buy something you don't need or really even want, then how much you "save" on it is irrelevant. You are not saving; you are spending. The money is probably wasted because the purchase is not connected to your needs or goals.

WASTED TIME

In my experience, most teams are thoughtful with their monetary purchases. Imagine that your firm was about to buy a machine or software package that cost one thousand dollars. That outlay would not be a major purchase, even for a small company. Yet when the CEO asked, "What is this for, and why do we need it?" the buyer would be expected to produce a valid response. There would be an explicit, stated reason for investing those dollars in that way.

We often give less thought to how we spend time than to how we spend money. While we'd hesitate to make a $1,000 purchase without a good rationale, we might spend thousands of dollars' worth of our own time without giving comparable scrutiny to that investment.

Most businesses follow some manner of budgeting process, in which they allocate funds in accordance with obligations and priorities. We may follow a similar approach toward planning our time as we look at the days and weeks ahead. *But spending time is far more passive than spending money.* Without our making any decisions or taking any action, time marches on. If we don't actively connect our calendar and clock to our goals, our schedule from hour to hour can easily be driven by habit and precedent because "that's just what we do around here."

MISSED INNOVATION

If you were trying to define the opposite of innovation, you might land on "doing things the way they've been done in the past." Relying on precedent denies the chance to improve efficiency or raise quality.

We should note that innovation doesn't always bring savings, and conversely holding on to the ways of the past may not necessarily add measurable cost. A friend might have a preference for physical maps instead of using GPS directions; if he gets where he wants to go on time and enjoys the process, it's hard to argue that he "should" change just for the sake of modernity. Sometimes an entire segment of people resists innovation. As an example, attorneys were far slower to adopt word processing and email than many other fields (perhaps because they bill hourly?). But since the field was uniformly sluggish in this area, an individual attorney faced no glaring disadvantage due to old-fashioned methods of communication.

Slow adoption of new methods is costlier in competitive situations. Consider:

- The restaurant that resists using social media to communicate with its fans, and is less effective getting out messages of special events and promotions.

- The manufacturing company that doesn't adopt a new automated process, and finds that its competitors are able to deliver products less expensively because of reduced labor costs.

- The sports team that doesn't change its strategy after a rule change, and sees its competition beat them by taking advantage of the new rule.

Disengagement and Aimlessness

The greatest cost to inertia and thoughtlessness may be in team performance. The term "employee engagement" was coined in the mid-1990s. Since then, the topic has been deeply and widely explored. It seems self-evident that employees who understand and believe in the importance of their job will perform better, and numerous studies have demonstrated a positive correlation between high engagement and profitability.[19] (So if for some reason it's not intuitive that you can get more done with motivated and engaged people, just look at the data.)

Dan Pink puts it this way in his book *Drive:* "True motivation is driven by a feeling of purpose, that one's contributions matter." If anyone on your team has the sense that they are doing any activity simply because "that's the way it's done," then they don't know why their actions matter.

If your aim is to be as effective as possible, then every person on your team needs to understand the purpose and importance of his or her actions. They need to know why what they do matters. We'll spend the rest of this chapter asking and answering the question "Why are we doing this?"

Examining Why We Do What We Do

This chapter probably features the least controversial Expensive Sentence in our collection. When we discuss "We can probably do that ourselves" or "We're different," there are nuances to unpack, and scenarios when the sentences are useful. But few of you reading would defend a practice on the sole grounds of "that's how we do it here."

I've included "That's the way we've always done it" in this book because it may be the most Expensive Sentence that you never hear. It's likely that a reliance on precedent over purpose is having a greater impact on your team than you realize. (And unfortunately, if an Expensive Sentence falls in a forest and no one is there to hear the sound, it can still cost a bundle.)

We tend to believe that we are doing the right things the right way. That assumed confidence may rest on experience and prior success. But if we don't periodically examine our reasons, we may forget those reasons. If we did ask why more often—and if we answered candidly—we might hear the rationale "that's the way we've always done it."

WE DON'T LIKE TO ASK WHY

In many relationships, families, groups, and teams, the question "why" is rare and unpopular. Consider how often you hear these questions, and in what settings:

- Why are you doing that?

- Why are you doing it that way?

When children ask why too many times, peeved adults tell them "just because" or "ask me later" or "because I'm daddy, that's why." Later it's the parents' turn to ask why, as in "Zachary, why did you spill your spaghetti on the carpet?"

Could there be a good answer to that? Could Zachary reply "This party was getting dull" or "I hate that ugly carpet"? The truth is, the poor eight-year-old probably didn't plan to spill his spaghetti—it just kind of happened.

When we (as adults) are asked why, it can recall our own childhood versions of spilling the spaghetti. We might feel defensive, inferring that we've done something wrong. Indeed, the question "why?" can imply inexperience, ineptitude, inefficiency, or even bad intentions. Most of us don't like to be asked why, nor do we enjoy asking others.

WE MUST ASK WHY

"Why" demands an answer. It expects intention and rationale that sometimes don't exist. That occasional lack of rationale is the very reason it's so important to ask why. In an organizational setting, there should always be intention. Actions shouldn't be thoughtless or careless or happen by default; actions should advance goals.

For the record, I'm sure that I did ask the government client why they needed the extra levels of approval. My failure at that point was accepting the surface-level answer of "because those other people also need to approve the bills." I was too quick to check the box and say "of course they do!" when I needed to ask at least one more why.

It is always less work to accept the surface rationale and assume that things happen for valid reasons. But without examining rationale, we run the risk of wasting energy, time, and money… and even undermining our purpose. Asking why is essential to rooting out this Expensive Sentence.

On your team, do you welcome the why?

REPLACING PRECEDENT WITH PURPOSE

Inertia, precedent, and history make for squishy ground; it's easier to walk on a firm foundation of intention and purpose. Asking why provides an opportunity to improve the performance of everyone on the team as actions are challenged through the lens of strategy. If you are revisiting the rationale on your team, consider the steps below as a starting point.

STEP 1: START WITH THE PAIN

Problems often provide wonderful occasions to improve and to ask why. When you want to make sure your actions are connected to your purpose, you might as well start with something you have to fix anyway. Sometimes just making the connection to the purpose can solve a problem—or eliminate it.

I remember an unhappy client from my days leading operations. We gave them a monthly report they wanted, but we couldn't seem to get it right. Finally, my boss asked me why we were making a custom report for them. I answered with an Expensive Sentence casserole: "We've always done it. The customer is always right." I might have even thrown in "We can probably do that ourselves" and "It's too late to turn back now." But after thinking it through, we realized that we really didn't want to be in the custom report business for numerous reasons. Within a few months we developed a reporting tool that our customers could use themselves. The problem was solved and would never appear again because we took the time to examine why we were doing the activity before we fixed the problem.

If you have anything like a complaint-handling routine, bug checklist, or trouble-ticket system, it might be worth adding the question "why" to the process. Beyond asking why the problem arose, encourage your team to ask why they are even doing that function. If the connection to the purpose is evident, asking why will not add any time to the fix. If the connection is elusive, then the bug fix has raised a bigger question that should be answered.

STEP 2: ANSWER THE BIG QUESTIONS

After fixing the urgent problems and connecting them to a solid rationale, it's time to step back and consider the big picture: What is the purpose of your team?

If you have a company vision or mission statement handy, that may be helpful. But the point here is not to wordsmith an inspirational beacon, but to anchor your activities in answers to basic questions:

- Whom do you serve?
- What problems do you solve for those customers?
- How do you solve those problems?
- What do you do better than your competitors?
- How do you measure success?

If these questions generate debate and confusion, then company identity and strategy may be vague (at least to some on the team). It may be hard to move forward until you have short answers that all can rally around.

STEP 3: GET TACTICAL

After the first two steps, we are assuming that there are no figurative fires and that the team has a basic shared understanding of who it is and what it does. That backdrop will help to examine how time and resources are spent.

When team leaders invite others into an authentic discussion about whether the team is doing the right things the right way, there is usually plenty to talk about. The success of the discussion will depend on the tone set by the leaders. Defensiveness and perceived insecurity will squash input and limit any progress. Genuine openness and willingness to change will open the doors to great ideas and bring higher engagement. (See the Start/Stop/Continue model at the end of the chapter for one approach to this discussion.)

THE VALUE OF FRESH EYES AND CONSULTANTS

It can be hard to get enough distance from our work to know when to examine our rationale. Sometimes patterns and habits are so entrenched that we don't recognize them.

Adding someone new to the team can offer a priceless chance to learn, and that learning must be intentionally pursued. Every new person brings a fresh perspective and will notice things that old hands have become inured to. But it's also true that most people are reluctant to ask a lot of questions if they're "the new guy" or "the new gal."

So don't waste the opportunity of having fresh eyes—make it a point to explicitly ask any new teammates to share all of the observations and questions they have, and set the expectation that they will challenge the status quo. Otherwise, the new hire may walk around the organization for years saying "that's just the way we do things here," assuming a rationale when there is none.

Like new hires, outside consultants see things differently and are willing to challenge existing practices. Consultants are paid for that input and expected to criticize and observe. Giving new and existing team members the same expectation for critical thought and questioning can trim many dollars from the consulting budget.

RESETTING WITH A NEW GOAL

In *The Power of Habit,* Charles Duhigg writes about when the aluminum company Alcoa brought in Paul O'Neill as its new CEO. O'Neill brought a singular focus to safety at the company, putting that goal above everything else. He insisted that he be notified about every safety incident, no matter how small. Then company leaders would develop a plan to ensure that the accident would never happen again—even if it was due to human error.

Predictably, safety improved markedly under O'Neill and accidents nearly vanished. The man-bites-dog part of the story was that profits soared. Costs dropped dramatically, quality improved, and sales picked up. As a (perhaps) unintended consequence of safety obsession, every process in the company was scrutinized and made safer—as well as more efficient and predictable. Furthermore, communication between senior management and frontline workers improved dramatically. This led to innovation, as employees shared ideas for new products and better practices. It also undoubtedly led to better engagement, as management demonstrably conveyed the importance of worker safety.

The singular obsession with safety at Alcoa left no stone unturned in connecting actions with purpose. Other companies have emphasized innovation, customer service, operational excellence, and other values in a way that measured all activities in terms of how they contributed to a core value.

Asking Why at a Higher Level

A belief that "this is just the way we do things" can pervade an industry, country, or discipline so much that leaders are blindsided when someone tries a new approach. Military history is rife with examples in which one side inflicted terror by pursuing unthinkable innovations. This was the case in the first skirmish of the American Revolutionary war, when the well-trained, professional British army met an underequipped mishmash of new recruits under George Washington at Bunker Hill. Washington understood that he was at a disadvantage in numbers, in weapons, in ammunition, and in training. He may have been forced to innovate rather than rely upon warfare tactics as they had been taught and practiced for generations in Europe. The new approach was both shocking and effective, as related by Ron Chernow in the biography *Alexander Hamilton*:

> The British were unhinged by the colonists' unorthodox fighting style and shocking failure to abide by gentlemanly rules of engagement. One scandalized British soldier complained that the American riflemen "conceal themselves behind trees etc. till an opportunity presents itself of taking a shot at our advanced sentries, which done, they immediately retreat. What an unfair method of carrying on a war!"

"That's not fair—they can't do that!" may be an instinctive reaction we see others reject precedent and move ahead, leaving us behind. In the case of the British generals at Bunker Hill, this was not simply an Expensive Sentence but a deadly one.

Wise Replies to "That's the way we've always done it"

. . . .

There is opportunity when tradition, precedent, or inertia are revealed to be driving your actions. Seize those moments to connect with purpose and intention.

Responding Directly to Expensive Sentences

Fight language with better language. The responses below illustrate how an Expensive Sentence can be redirected and then used to spark a productive conversation.

> ❝ *Yes, that is the way we've done it before. I'm sure there were good reasons for that approach, too… but at the moment I'm not sure what they would be. What if there's a better way to do it?"*

> ❝ *I'm all for tradition, but of course we want our business to be driving toward our goals, not just based on tradition."*

> ❝ *So 'That's the way we've always done it'… is that a reason, or an excuse?"*

> ❝ *Do you think our biggest competitor does it that way? Why, or why not?"*

> ❝ *Is that the answer we want to give to our board or our investors, or for that matter our best customer? If not, then we have a great opportunity now to make sure we are doing the right thing for the right reasons, and not just defaulting to what is familiar or convenient."*

QUESTIONS FOR REFLECTION AND DISCUSSION

We all drift from intentional action. If you want your team to be more thoughtful and connected to purpose, ask and discuss some of the questions below:

Organizational

Why is your team organized like it is?

Why are job titles worded the way they are?

Why is the reporting structure set up as it is?

Why do we use vendors for certain functions?

Why do we do certain activities in-house with staff?

Communication & Protocol

Why are meetings one hour? Could they be a half-hour by default?

Why do/don't all meetings have an agenda?

Why are staff meetings on Monday (Tuesday, etc.)?

Why are the meetings scheduled at a certain frequency?

Why do some people attend meetings and others do not?

Why do we answer email?

Why do we email instead of call?

Why do we travel instead of use videoconferences?

Office Practices

Why do certain people sit where they do?

Why does the development team go to lunch together?

Why do some people telecommute, and others come to the office?

Why do we go to conferences?

Why do we advertise in a certain way?

Why do/don't we get certain training?

While we're rolling with questions, let's remember that acting out of default and losing connection to the purpose is not just something that happens at work. Consider additional questions for other arenas:

School

Why do our teachers need a certain specific education?

Why is the school day a certain length?

Why do we get some days off as holidays?

Why do we take tests?

Why are there report cards?

Faith

Why are scriptures read? (Or why are they not read?)

Why do people sit where they sit?

Why do we sing music?

Why do we sing the particular songs that we do?

Why do certain rituals happen on certain days?

Why are the messages the length that they are?

Family

Why do we take vacations?

Why do we travel for the holidays?

Why do/don't we spend time with other families?

Why do we live in this area?

Why are different kids in different specific bedrooms?

Why do/don't we eat meals together?

Why do we do what we do on Saturday/Sunday?

Why does mom work? Why does dad work?

Why do/don't we watch TV together?

Why is/isn't there music playing in the house?

Personal Habits

Why do I use social media?

Why do I check my email when I check it?

Why do I answer the phone without knowing who it is?

Why do I watch the TV shows I watch?

Why do I listen to the music I listen to?

Why do I spend my free time as I do?

If reading any of these questions caused you to feel defensive or ashamed, I can promise you that I wasn't thinking of your situation when I wrote them down. (Take a deep breath and smile.) There's no need to be threatened, but you may have an opportunity to revisit your habits and recalibrate.

Discussing these matters with a family or a team is a chance to build engagement and ownership as you affirm your values and clarify your goals. In our families or religious institutions, many of us expect tradition and find it comforting. That is fine, but consider that questioning the origin and purpose of certain activities does not inherently challenge or diminish them. If anything, it may strengthen your own connection to those activities to think through why they are done.

EXERCISES TO REPLACE INERTIA WITH PURPOSE

Discussions of purpose and answering why may be easier in the specific context provided by these exercises.

EXERCISE: FIGHT INERTIA WITH "STOP, START, CONTINUE"

One simple and effective way to reconnect with purpose is to perform the "Start, Stop, and Continue" exercise. This is most effective when a team does it together, but it begins with each member individually answering the following open-ended questions:

- What are we doing now as a team that we should we *stop* doing?

- What are we not doing that we should we *start* doing?

- What are we doing now that we should we *continue* doing?

When presenting these to your team, it's better not to give guidance or set parameters to the answers. The questions speak for themselves.

After individuals have answered these questions, the group compares answers. The findings might illuminate clear areas where there is strong agreement to change course, or they may uncover substantial disagreements on the best way forward. Any answers provide a way to connect actions to goals and ensure that the team is not moving simply from inertia.

Exercise: The Six Whys

Sometimes connecting actions to purpose is as simple as asking the question "Why?" When I led a CEO peer group, one of the most popular leadership exercises was called the Six Whys. Here's how it worked. I'd start by asking people in the group what they were doing at work yesterday at 3:00. (The hour didn't really matter; the point was to pick a specific part of the workday.) Then they would answer:

"Yesterday at 3:00 I was writing an email to Chris." Then I'd ask:

Why is that important?

Because Chris is our tech lead, and I was telling him how to improve a piece of our interface.

Why is that important? (Second ask.)

Because that part of the interface was slow.

Why is that important? (Number three – now it's sort of annoying.)

Because if our software is slow, the clients are less likely to use it.

Why is that important? (Hang in there...)

Because when the clients use our software, they get better results and actually save time.

Why is that important? (Aha, now we're getting somewhere.)

Because if the clients can do this part of their job faster and better, they don't have to worry about it as much.

Why is that important? (Here's the payoff!)

So our clients can get to the more important parts of their business or more enjoyable parts of their lives.

The email to Chris was nothing special; quite often, whatever we were doing at 3:00 yesterday was something seemingly mundane. Yet in a few short questions, we connected that mundane action to the entire reason the company existed and its purpose in serving customers.

The Six Whys exercise often serves as encouragement that reveals the meaning behind our drudgery. It can also raise more questions if the answers are less than satisfactory. Either path is useful as long as the answers are honest—and if we are willing to confront those actions that we do out of default.[20]

PART 3

DEBUNKING THE
SCARCE MYTHS

Is there enough?

Do you have the time, money, and resources you need to do what you want to do?

Or are your decisions clouded by shortages or a fear of lack?

At the core of economics is scarcity: the principle that resources are limited and insufficient to provide for all human needs and wants. Some resources are more *scarce* than others, and the more limited a useful resource is, the more costly it is likely to become.

Common sense validates the principle of scarcity. For example, gold is far less available than wood, and therefore gold is more valuable than wood. Or consider real estate: at any given moment, there is a finite number of four-bedroom houses for sale in Sacramento. If that number gets smaller, the prices will increase.

It's also self-evident that resources are limited. There is only so much food in our pantries, and only so much money in our bank accounts. That means we can't feed everyone or buy everything.

But a closer look at scarcity shows that it is not absolute. Gold is more valuable than wood in the marketplace, but less valuable if you are trying to build a chair or start a fire. Different situations bring different values for the same resources.

And while we can't do everything with our resources, who is to say that we can't do enough?

Indeed, enough is an elusive finish line. When the world's richest man was asked, "How much money is enough?" he reportedly answered, "Just a little bit more." Even if John D. Rockefeller didn't utter those words, many others have lived by them.

It's not just the greedy and ambitious who want more, though. We might consider whether our own standards of financial sufficiency are solid or shifting. Would our answer to "How much is enough?" be different today from what we said a decade or two ago? We may believe that our assets are insufficient, yet someone on the other side of the globe—or the other side of town—might deem them luxurious.

The moving target of "enough" extends beyond money. Consider technology: the television set that was fantastically futuristic ten years ago became commonplace five years ago and is now considered old. Our computers' processing speed and storage capacity would have been more than we ever needed ten years ago; now they seem barely adequate.

Here's the point: scarcity is not black and white, but a range of gray tones driven by two questions:

- How valuable are our resources?

- How much is sufficient?

The answers to these questions are not scientific, they are subjective. Scarcity, then, is not imposed solely by economic facts. Scarcity is often a matter of perspective. In other words, the answer to the question "Do we have enough?" depends as much on our perception and thoughts as it does on our possessions.

More than Just Blowing Sunshine

At this point, you might feel like you've wandered from an economics textbook to the self-help section of a bookstore. That's OK—those books sell better anyway, because more people find them helpful. And thinkers from widely divergent worldviews have reached similar conclusions about the importance of perception. Here are some labels used for this idea in different circles:

- The power of positive thinking (popular psychology)

- Manifestation, or the law of attraction (success literature)

- The prosperity gospel, or "name it and claim it" (Christian lifestyle)

- Visualization (sports psychology)

These concepts all feature the decisive power of thinking and suggest that one's beliefs about one's circumstances are often more important than the circumstances themselves.

Maybe that insight sheds light on the surprising words of Jesus recorded in Matthew 13:

"Whoever has will be given more, and they will have an abundance. Whoever does not have, even what they have will be taken from them."[21]

At first glance, this curt assessment of the "haves" versus the "have-nots" is a bit tough to read coming from a moral teacher. It seems like a cynical admission that the rich will get richer and the poor will get poorer.

Or is it a choice? Is it a challenge?

We'll see in this section that we do have a choice when it comes to scarcity. We can accept it or we can reject it. If we seek abundance, we can find it. Moreover, we will see that achieving more abundance is not a mystical or spiritual pursuit, but can be done by combining common-sense insight with practical steps.

Finding Abundance, Debunking Scarcity

The first step in improving things is to stop making them worse. If the right thoughts can help us see more abundance, then it's also true that the wrong perspective can magnify scarcity. Negative thinking can add to our problems, as we're reminded by the fretful old man who rued:

I've had many troubles in this life. Most of them never happened.

We can create scarcity by worrying about problems that don't materialize. We can imagine the negative scenarios to the point where they become self-fulfilling prophecies.

Have you known anyone to gaze into a full pantry and say "there's nothing here to eat," or turn on a 200-channel satellite TV receiver and conclude "there's nothing to watch"? We are all prone to discount or ignore the options in front of us and instead see scarcity. This happens at home and it happens at work, to individuals and to teams. In this section we will examine several specific myths of scarcity that may be costing your team far more than you realize:

- **"WE CAN'T AFFORD TO LET HIM GO."** Has an employee, a vendor, or a friend ever become essential to you? Is anyone in your life or business irreplaceable? We'll unpack the reasons behind "indispensable" and see that great help is often not as scarce as it seems.

- **"THE CUSTOMER IS ALWAYS RIGHT."** This proverb is nearly sacred in some circles as a beacon to excellent service. But it can lead to cost and confusion, and ironically it can leave us with many unhappy customers. The root is often a belief in the scarcity of paying customers.

- **"WE CAN PROBABLY DO THAT OURSELVES."** What seems to be prudent thrift can lead to cost and mediocrity. Yet teams often take on too many tasks because they overlook the abundance of expertise outside of their organization or because they are confused about which of their resources are most scarce.

Each of these sentences has a connection to truth, but each one also has the potential to mislead people and derail decisions. By rewriting these sentences, we can turn scarcity into abundance.

Before LeBron James and before Michael Jordan, the greatest super-star in basketball was Julius "Dr. J." Erving. Erving had a seemingly miraculous knack for finding ways to the basket where other players could not. One interviewer asked him about his flamboyance and incredible moves. He answered that his approach was similar to that of others, with one exception:

> "When handling the ball, I always looked for daylight. Maybe I could see daylight that a lot of other players couldn't see."[22]

Let's see the daylight and fight the scarcity.

CHAPTER 7

"WE CAN'T AFFORD TO LET HIM GO"

"Nobody else can do what they do."

"We'd be sunk without her."

"I am afraid to break up with him."

"No one else has their technology."

IF YOU HAVE EVER COMPLETED A LARGE JIGSAW PUZZLE, THEN YOU KNOW the immense satisfaction of putting that last small piece of contoured cardboard in its place. Everything is where it should be, and you can stand back and behold the beautiful picture. All is serene and sublime.

It's a very different feeling when you near completion but realize that you are missing one piece out of a thousand. Panic and despair set in because you know that only one piece can complete the picture, and without that exact shape and design, the job can never be finished. The piece is irreplaceable.

Too often, we view our teams as jigsaw puzzles with a collection of individual and irreplaceable pieces. Of course, it's a joy to work with people who consistently perform highly. That's a good thing and worthy of affirmation (as in, "Where would we be without Joanne?"). But danger lurks when someone graduates from the "highly valued" zone and enters "irreplaceable" territory. When any component of the team becomes essential, the team is vulnerable. That's true whether it's a fellow employee, a consultant, a vendor, or even a product or technology. The belief in irreplaceability sets the stage for a number of Expensive Sentences:

- "We're paying them too much, I know, but they are the only vendor with that technology."

- "Yes, he's a pain and doesn't really fit our culture, but he knows our systems inside-out."

- "No, the clients don't like her, but she's the acknowledged leader in the field."

- "It's a clunky system, but it's the only way to get our data processed."

These sentences don't simply reflect tradeoffs or a realistic cost of doing business. They imply that the subject of the sentence cannot be replaced.

THE COST OF PERCEIVED IRREPLACEABILITY

Indispensable is often a supercharged synonym for expensive. The potential costs when someone "can't be replaced" include money, quality, business continuity, and team unity. All of these costs are rooted in scarcity.

It's important to remember that perceived scarcity has the same effect as actual scarcity. When we believe that certain people are so specifically qualified that they cannot be replaced, we are assigning them the highest value of scarcity.

Scarcity is a beautiful thing in romantic movies when the actor cries out, "You're the only one for me!" In those climactic moments, the hero is the essence of transparency and vulnerability. He entrusts his fate to the mercy of his beloved, who has the power to receive him or reject him. It's good drama, and finding your one-and-only soulmate is a lovely thing. But is that how you want to position yourself in the business world? "She's the only one who can do the job" is an explicit declaration of scarcity. To decide (consciously or not) that a vendor or employee is irreplaceable is to accept a one-way exclusive agreement. It's akin to saying, "You can do what you want and charge what you want, and I will continue to work with you." (Cue the romantic background music… and hold onto your wallet.)

This one-sided relationship suggests a different kind of movie scene: a bank robbery in a classic Western. In fact, economists use the term *holdup* to describe the dynamic in which someone is essential. Holdup occurs when one party has the power to demand virtually anything from the other party. In other common language, it's called being "held hostage." Even a mild version of a holdup can cost us time and opportunities; and of course it can mean that we pay more. As we'll explore later in this chapter, paying a premium can be a perfectly sensible thing to do; but not when it's based on a false premise of scarcity.

THREATS TO QUALITY

The impact of an irreplaceable teammate or vendor doesn't end on the invoice. A more subtle danger relates to quality.

When someone on the team believes that "we can't replace Anderson," it implies that Anderson has been doing an excellent job. After all, a mediocre employee or vendor would be easy to replace. But just as you shouldn't claim to understand market pricing without obtaining current quotes, it can be misleading to assume that someone's performance is top-notch based on limited information.

189

For some jobs, performance standards are readily available and easily measured. In those cases, success can be substantiated with data: sales results, speed, customer satisfaction surveys, or other hard numbers. Where success is more qualitative and subjective, there is a greater danger of losing sight of quality; especially if the person performing it carries the designation of "irreplaceable."

Blind Spots

When I work with a company leader who waxes poetic about the unequalled wisdom and skill of their favorite consultant, I have to exercise self-control. In my gut I know that an idealized opinion of any vendor is dangerous, and that there's a good chance that within a week I could find someone to do a comparable job for 30 percent less money. But telling a CEO that you can easily replace her pet vendor is like telling a mother that her child is ugly: it doesn't end well, regardless of the truth.

So the direct approach won't be useful. Instead, I might ask if it's possible that the vendor has blind spots. Could there be some new developments in the field that he is not aware of?

Even this nudge is often resisted; it can be hard to imagine that successful people would be unaware of anything important in their field. But let's consider three facts from the world of sports:

1. The greatest golfers in the world have coaches.

2. The first indoor game of hockey was played in 1875.

3. The first time an NHL goalie wore a hockey mask full-time was 1959.

From these facts we will draw two important lessons. First (from Fact 1), even professionals realize that they can improve with someone else's help. An outside perspective always sees something different, and even the best performers realize that they don't know everything and need to keep improving. (Maybe that's why they became the best performers.)

Second, the obvious can be elusive. This lesson is drawn from Facts 2 and 3. For the better part of a century, hockey goalies faced rock-hard pucks flying at their faces at 90 miles per hour without any protection. How many black eyes and missing teeth would any player have to endure before concluding that there might be a better way? Yet sometimes even those closest to the problem miss a simple solution.

We don't know what we don't know—and neither do other people. It's no insult to suggest that someone can't see everything that happens in their industry; it is simply acknowledging the truth. When you overestimate an expert's knowledge or perspective, you risk missing out on recent developments or other helpful points of view.

THREATS TO BUSINESS CONTINUITY

Someone who is irreplaceable cannot be replaced. That's an obvious statement, but it reveals another challenge caused by believing that someone is essential: what do you do if you lose that person?

Years ago it was commonplace to ask, "What if George were hit by a bus? What would we do then?" Or if you prefer a less gruesome fantasy, you can ask: "What if George wins the lottery and decides that our workplace is less fun than an island paradise?"

Losing a key player raises concerns about numerous valid issues: continuity of business, providing for families, maintaining customer relationships, and others. Not every team needs or can afford a perfect backup plan to handle every departure, but it is useful to think through the realistic steps of what would happen.

One of the benefits of contingency-planning is that it opens up alternatives. When we are forced to face unpleasant possibilities and define our options, we realize we have more than we thought. (It's worth noting that the opposite of a holdup—and the cure for virtually every Expensive Sentence—is having more options.)

The Cost of the Wrong Fit

How do you calculate the price of something that is priceless? What is the replacement value of something that is essential?

When everything runs smoothly, these questions are moot because the costs remain low. But when friction starts near someone who is seen as indispensable, things get messy. Because the person's perceived value is off the charts, the acceptable cost associated with that person will also be very high. This imbalance may cause a company to pay too much or agree to uneven terms, or it may cause a team's leader to compromise on strategy or values. At worst, keeping the wrong person around can cause the right people to leave.

I witnessed firsthand just how expensive it can be when one person can't be replaced.

Too Wrong, Too Long

Years ago I worked at a small company that offered a mix of services and technology solutions. Our niche required us to work with an obscure computer programming language that was largely obsolete but still used in our clients' old systems. No one on our team was skilled in this language, so our Chief Technology Officer, Bob, scoured résumés looking for someone who could help.

One day, Bob burst into my office with a huge smile on his face. "I think I've found him!" he said, and he showed me the résumé of someone who had a perfect technical background for our needs. His name was Louis. He lived several states away from us, but we arranged to have Louis come and interview. We hired him as a consultant, with an arrangement in which he traveled to work with us some of the time and worked remotely some of the time.

Louis had a quirky personality. This was not unique among technical talent, but as the months went on, we learned that some of Louis's quirks were grating on his teammates. Then Louis became involved in conflicts with several of his teammates, and it was clear that he was mostly at fault. Things escalated to the point where two people on the technical team had closed-door sessions with Bob to complain about Louis. At this point, the CEO and I had a discussion with Bob. It went sort of like this:

"Louis seems to be causing problems. Are we sure he's the right fit?"

"Look, I know he's got issues. But he's doing amazing work, and no one else on the team knows the programming language. We can't afford to let him go."

Two months later, things had gotten worse, and we had the same conversation. We pressed Bob on Louis's unique skills, since they were the main justification to keep him.

"Couldn't one of the other developers learn from Louis? At this point, could they pick up from what he's done?" Bob said it would set the company back many months and hurt our ability to serve our clients.

Another four months went on, and the behavior from Louis became more problematic. Several people told Bob that they would not work directly with Louis. We changed reporting structures so that Louis had less contact with other teammates. He had become poison to the culture.

Management discussed Louis again several times, but in each case Bob—who as the Chief Technology Officer was the authority on all things related to development—insisted that we could not afford to lose Louis.

Finally, we were forced to act. Louis acted in a way that violated company policy and exposed us to possible lawsuits. Our attorney and HR lead told us that it was crystal clear: we could not continue to employ Louis without assuming an unacceptable level of legal risk. Bob reluctantly agreed, and we removed Louis from the team.

Now with Louis gone, we faced what had been considered unthinkable: we had to move forward without the only person in the region who had the expertise to perform this critical function for our company. So what happened?

You can probably guess that we survived. For about six weeks, there was a mad scramble to figure things out, and then someone else on the team was able to pick up Louis's workload. At that point people were asking, "Why didn't we get rid of him sooner?"

It's hard for me to overstate the pain and drama associated with having Louis on the team: the whispers, the raised eyebrows, the lunch conversations dominated by his latest antics, the indignation toward company leadership for keeping him around so long. I can't convey how bad it was without spending too many words and sharing too many details; but if you have ever been through a similar experience, you probably understand.

Damage to culture is not the only threat posed by keeping a so-called essential person around. The costs of your essential player may weaken your profitability or may threaten the very existence of your team. In any case, an employee or vendor that "you can't afford to lose" may be costing you more than you realize.

THREATS TO TEAM UNITY

When I was working with the toxic teammate, a business mentor told me, "When you realize that the wrong person is on the team, it's always too late." By "too late" he meant that the mismatch has already led to unnecessary cost and waste by the time it is recognized.

Any personnel move deserves appropriate care and deliberation. But delays in dismissing the wrong person can cause teams to prolong numerous costs that ripple throughout the team, farther than we might realize.

When a teammate isn't getting his job done, there is a direct cost in productivity. When a teammate takes care of his tasks but negatively affects others on the team, there are indirect costs in productivity. These costs are just as real as the direct costs, and we can identify the ways they add up:

- **TEAM FRICTION** — When people are arguing with each other, they are not contributing to the productivity of the team.

- **GOSSIP** — When one teammate's actions cause others to talk, gossip time detracts from performance.

- **DISTRACTION** — If anyone on a team believes that the wrong person is on the team, and that the person's status may be in jeopardy, the unsettled personnel matters can detract from their focus.

- **MISTRUST OF LEADERSHIP** — A collateral cost of a bad fit who stays is the team's belief that leadership doesn't care or isn't aware. Neither of these is helpful.

These costs have a combined effect that is like a tax on the enterprise. There may be a specific reason that you think you "can't afford to let him go," but are you sure you can afford to have him stay?

Team cohesion and engagement can be difficult to measure. One framework is to think of your normal productivity as a number. That number gets multiplied by a coefficient based on the health of your organization. When everything is healthy, the coefficient is 100 percent. But when someone on the team has a consistently negative effect, it brings that number down. Anything below 100 percent hurts you, and the more intense the situation, the lower that number goes.

If the wrong person stays on the team, the low number lingers and the expense grows. Just as we sometimes overestimate the value of one person's contribution, we are prone to underestimate the cost of a bad fit.

Evaluating a Teammate's Fit

Legendary General Electric CEO Jack Welch understood the full cost of having the wrong player on a team. Welch also appreciated the conundrum that arises when this wrong player is also a strong individual contributor. He describes a simplified way of evaluating teammates based on two dimensions: numbers and values.

If someone doesn't share the values of the organization and can't make enough of a contribution, it's clear that the person is not a fit and should be dismissed. The decision is just as clear on the positive side: a teammate who has the values and hits the numbers is an easy "yes." When someone has the right values but struggles to make the numbers, Welch says the best path is to work with that person to try to improve his performance—give him every opportunity to succeed before you conclude that he doesn't measure up.[23]

The most challenging scenario occurs when the performance is strong (numbers) but the values don't match. If an employee is bringing in revenue or otherwise making a strong quantifiable contribution, team leadership will be inclined to keep that person and excuse other shortcomings (just as we did with Louis). But Welch is emphatic that employees who don't fit team culture must be let go. The cost is harder to see, but it is extremely high. If you sacrifice your team culture because "you can't afford to let him go," you will destroy the integrity of your team.

Understanding and Challenging Irreplaceability

It's helpful to analyze why we get stuck in the idea that someone or something is irreplaceable. We'll see that just a few reasons—either we think we can't replace someone's expertise, technology, relationships, or talent—cover nearly all of the cases. When you can isolate the reason, it's easier to understand and then challenge the notion that you can't afford to let that person or thing go.

Irreplaceable Expertise

A person's specific, relevant expertise may make him seem essential. That expertise might be very local and specific to your company: "Raymond was here when they built the database—he knows it inside and out." The expertise can be global and widely useful: "Sally has a better understanding of the oil market than anyone on Wall Street."

Here again, perception is far more important than reality. Team leaders can develop the idea of irreplaceable expertise even when dozens of potential hires or vendors could step in without missing a beat. Information technology professionals, strategic consultants, and coaches are among those most frequently prized because of their specific expertise, despite the fact that those are highly competitive fields with an abundance of fabulously qualified people.

Sometimes the source of this belief can be flawed attitudes about expertise and skill. Expertise should not be seen as fixed or unattainable; a learning organization is constantly acquiring and transferring expertise. Expertise should be documented and shared. When expertise is hoarded, it puts an organization at risk.

The "Tech Guy" Who Can't Be Replaced

It may be a coincidence, but many of the cases where I have seen "we can't replace him" firsthand have been related to technology. (And since these technical experts have all been male, I'll keep using the pronoun "him" with your permission.) It's happened three times with developers, once with a network administrator, and once with an outsourced vendor.

In four of these cases, the loudest voice protesting that "we can't afford to let him go" came from the corner office: the CEO. This may be a specific vulnerability related to IT. When a CEO doesn't understand how the technology works, those who do understand it have the potential to create a certain mystery. Technology is so powerful it can seem like magic, and those who control it can have the sway of sorcerers. It's worth asking the question: what if your tech wizard disappeared?

In one small company I worked with, this vulnerability devolved into a situation that was not unlike blackmail. The "irreplaceable" tech guy began abusing his position. He would spend fewer and fewer hours in the office, and when he was there, he was often playing video games. He knew that the CEO was afraid to fire him, and he acted accordingly. He was drunk on power.

The antidotes to mystery and magic are visibility and exposure. When you understand how a magician does his tricks, the mystery evaporates. You might even figure out how to do the trick yourself.

IRREPLACEABLE TECHNOLOGY OR PRODUCTS

Companies often present their offerings as the vanguard of technological progress and unique in the marketplace. Their claims are sometimes true and often effective, especially for buyers who like to have the latest and greatest. When we hear the words "proprietary" or "industry-leading" or "next-generation" used to justify why a team just has to use a specific vendor, the basis is probably technology or a product.

The assertion that "we need this product" or "we have to use this technology" should never be accepted on its surface. The natural follow-up questions are critical: why do you need it, and what does it do that is essential? Without challenging your teammates in an adversarial way, you can ask them to help you understand three things:

- What function is required, and why?

- What features are valuable, and why?

- What features are preferred, and why?

Note that the assumption behind the questions is that while some features are helpful, none is actually required. Every tool has a function: for example, a hammer has the function of pounding in a nail. That's what a hammer absolutely has to do. The feature of a handle on a hammer is valuable because it helps generate leverage and power for the hammer, and that saves time. Padding on the hammer handle is preferred because it reduces blisters and allows a worker to hammer longer. Every feature must advance a goal to be valuable.

The product itself is only a means to an end; it is a tool used to create results leading toward a team goal. When we get fixated on a specific technology or product, it often means we have taken our eyes off the result for which the tool was needed in the first place.

IRREPLACEABLE RELATIONSHIPS

An employee may have certain contacts that are valuable to the business. This can be particularly true in law, marketing, and some areas of consulting in which clients are often more loyal to the individual practitioner than to the firm that employs her. Are you afraid that if a certain employee or vendor steps away, paying customers will follow? If so, those relationships are a basis for this person's being seen as essential.

Another flavor of relationships is access. You may value an advertising partner because that company owns publications that reach your target market; that is, the partner provides access to that group. A club or trade association might be especially useful because it provides occasions to connect with likely partners or customers.

Good relationships take time to develop and cannot be bought, so it is wise to view them as assets and assign appropriate value. Still, there are times when relationships can be overvalued. When you're gauging the value, it again helps to distinguish between resources and results. Relationships are a resource that can be immensely valuable, but they are rarely a business goal in themselves. (The obvious exception is customer relationships, which often are a business goal, but even those are not irreplaceable as we'll explore in the next chapter.)

TALENTS OR INTANGIBLES

In most of the cases when someone is viewed as indispensable, it will be because of expertise, technology, or relationships. If none of those fit, there may be some quality that is simply hard to define. This could be some sort of intangible—maybe an employee is somehow the glue that keeps the team together, or perhaps there's a vendor that just seems to bring great performance out of your team.

As a personal preference, it may be fine to prefer the coffee barista who has a certain *je ne sais quoi*. But remember, that's just a fancy French way to say, "I don't know what." In a team setting, any reason for a preference should be written down and defensible. Take the time to name that intangible, and evaluate whether it really is a valid basis for a preference.

A Word of Warning

If you can't identify what makes the person irreplaceable after reviewing the possibilities above, there is some reason for caution. When business relationships don't seem to make sense on the surface, there may be a reason that they do make sense that is not widely known.

I worked with a company vice president who refused to change telecom providers because the incumbent vendor owned a box suite at the arena and was generous with hockey tickets. In another case, a beloved sales rep was known for taking team members to expensive lunches several times a year.

Free lunches and game tickets are dodgy support for business decisions, but sometimes vendors are favored for more egregious reasons. Unidentifiable reasons for "irreplaceable" relationships could extend into inappropriate personal relationships, extracurricular business dealings, kickbacks, or some other illicit activity. Any of those scenarios could have devastating personal and professional consequences for the culprits and innocent victims alike, so the situations must not be ignored. Inform authorities and proceed carefully if you stumble into this kind of unhappy mess.

When it's OK to Pay More than You Have to

We don't need to look far to see how scarcity and holdups combine to raise prices. When we pay full retail for the newest mobile phone or accept an expert consultant's exorbitant hourly rate, we are accepting the terms that a scarce resource demands. But is that a bad thing?

Paying more doesn't always equate to a holdup. There are times when we choose to pay a premium for a better product. We may buy tickets to see our favorite singer in concert or eat at a high-end restaurant despite the fact that there are much less expensive options for entertainment or dining. A company may pay an above-market rate for a talented employee, consultant, or vendor.

It's not necessarily wrong to pay a premium. Here are two rules to make sure you are not a victim of a holdup:

1. Know the premium you are paying

2. Define why the premium is worth it

Know the Premium

One of the most common objections to pursuing savings is the defense that "they may cost more, but they're worth it -- you get what you pay for." Another variant is "I wouldn't change vendors just to save 10 percent." These are usually Expensive Sentences.

It's perfectly valid to choose to pay a 10 percent premium. But my follow-up questions are: Are you sure it's only 10 percent you are overpaying? How do you know? What if the number were 50 percent... then would you change vendors?

If your gut tells you that you might be overpaying your IT consultant (or anyone else), don't repress it. Obey your instinct and find that premium by checking the marketplace. Once you get two or three other written quotes that are comparable, you will know whether you are paying above-market rates and how much that premium is. Without recent quotes in writing, you don't know your premium; you are only guessing.

Justify the Premium

The second principle of paying a premium is to define why you are doing so. If you and your date are enjoying the concert, it may be enough to say, "I just love Elton John." That's your money and your choice.

In a team context, the premium should be justified by connecting the extra benefit to a goal. Are you paying this person more because her expertise will allow you to launch your product more quickly? Because his training will lift the skill of your team, leading to more satisfied customers? Because her knowledge will save you time and reduce operational cost? Because having him on the team lowers your risk?

When you combine an understanding of the premium with an awareness of other real options, then you are not in a box. Which sentence would you rather say:

A: "We're overpaying Jill, but we can't afford to let her go."

B: "I know we're paying 20 percent more for Jill's services than we would with the other vendor, but this year she is worth that premium because of her specific expertise and her knowledge of our enterprise. That will increase our speed and lower our costs in other areas."

You can see how Sentence B has replaced scarcity with specific knowledge and valid reasons. It usually doesn't take too much work to get from A to B, but it's a move from guesswork to solid fact-based judgment. In some cases, that process will reveal a greater difference in cost—and perhaps an opportunity to improve quality as well.

THE VALUE OF WELL-PLACED PRAISE

While we're acknowledging that there are times when a known premium is worth paying, let's also allow that we can go too far in applying the concept that everyone is replaceable. After all, one way to avoid the Expensive Sentence "we can't afford to let him go" would be to constantly remind people that they are highly expendable. ("Watch your back, Wilson. There are a dozen blokes on the street who would love your job!") But that would bring other costs in fear, insecurity, and other team dynamics; it's probably not the path to a winning culture.

Verbal praise can be motivational and rewarding. It has the power to heal relationships. If your style is to be encouraging and generous with words, don't stop. But consider two perspectives: what do you really believe, and what is the object of your praise likely to believe? To this subject, I offer two cautions:

First, don't say any words that someday may not be true. It would have roughly the same short-term effect to say "Bill, your contribution has been extraordinary" or to say "Bill, we could never do this without you." But the latter statement could be interpreted as a promise of perpetual employment.

Second, take the occasion of appreciating someone to examine what you really believe. Is that person really someone you could not do without?

Here's a test that usually will reveal the truth. Imagine that the person came to you and asked if you had a minute to speak privately. She then sheepishly said that as much as she's enjoyed working with your team, a new opportunity has arisen that she feels compelled to pursue.

Would you break out into a sweat? Would your heart race? If your reaction surpasses disappointment and rises to the level of panic, you probably believe that this person would be very hard or perhaps impossible to replace. That may be a signal that it's time to develop some additional options.

Overcoming the Scarcity Mindset

The fear behind "We can't afford to let him go" can spiral and cause more fear. When President Franklin Roosevelt cautioned that "the only thing we have to fear is fear itself," he could have been talking about this Expensive Sentence.

If we believe that our success is dependent on any one link in the chain, it's only natural to overvalue that link and be afraid of losing it. The remedy is taking action: getting specific and creating options.

Finding More Options—Internet Advertising

Fear nearly destroyed a company I worked with.

The company was a niche internet retailer. It found all of its customers through web advertising on two specific websites. The company was struggling financially, and when we looked at the numbers, I saw that its advertising expenses were the largest line item—even bigger than payroll.

When I asked the CEO what his options were for advertising, he said, "I don't have any options. There's really nowhere else I can go to find customers." I then asked if he had negotiated his pricing.

"I can't negotiate with them; they're my only source of business. I just have to pay what they charge."

It took some time to work through these Expensive Sentences, but finally we decided to conduct a simple Request for Quote with the two websites. Our goal was to get better pricing. We figured that even without much competition, we had two possible incentives for the websites to cooperate: First, the advertising was split 70/30 between the sites, so we could offer more volume to either of them. Second, we could try committing to a longer term and larger volume over time.

As we were preparing to send our Request for Quote to the two websites, the CEO learned some interesting news: site A had just bought site B. So now instead of buying from a duopoly, we had only one supplier. Or that's certainly what it felt like.

Fear raised its head. The CEO didn't even want to try the RFQ for fear of angering the company behind the website. "There's no one else we can use for advertising," he said. "What if they raise our prices?"

I challenged the CEO on his perception of scarcity. Was it really true that if those two websites did not exist he would be out of business?

He admitted, "Well, no; I guess I'd figure out something."

We realized that the time to figure out something was at hand. I walked to the whiteboard and picked up a marker, and we started to brainstorm other ways to get customers.

I asked if he could send them direct mail. He said that was a terrible idea, way too expensive. But I wrote it up on the board anyway. We continued brainstorming.

What about advertising on general sites, instead of these sites that cater to your customers? Well, he said that probably would be too expensive, too.

How about keyword advertising that showed up when people did internet searches? Maybe that could work.

What about print advertising in some magazines that cater to your prospects? Yes, he admitted, some of his competitors did that and it might actually work.

The CEO mulled over these options for a few days and came up with some others that seemed feasible. Finally, it was time to take action. The CEO called his advertising supplier—who now was essentially the only player in the market—and spoke from a position of strength.

> "It's been great working together, but the economics are not working for me. I'm looking at some other ways to reach my customers, but if you have the ability to be flexible, I could possibly make a longer-term commitment to your company. If not, we'll part friends."

The net result was a savings of 19 percent with the same supplier. Since this was the largest expense for the company, a 19 percent savings dramatically changed the financial picture. About a year later, the CEO sold the company.

Breaking Out of Fear With Options

There are two important lessons from the internet advertising story that can help us all escape holdup: First, everything changed when the CEO believed that he had other viable options. Second, the path to good options often starts with bad options. It's a simple progression:

NO OPTIONS ▶ BAD OPTIONS ▶
ACCEPTABLE OPTIONS ▶ GOOD OPTIONS

Sometimes you'll be lucky and the great alternatives will simply appear. More often, you'll go through a process to move from "he's the only one for the job" or "they're the only vendor we can use" to a brighter scenario of having multiple good options. The first step may be writing down ideas that really don't seem feasible, but go ahead and write them down anyway. There is power in the process: better options will emerge.

WISE REPLIES TO "**WE CAN'T AFFORD TO LET HIM GO**"

. . . .

The next time you hear "we can't afford to let him go," or "she's irreplaceable" or "it's the only product like that on the market" or some other outgrowth of perceived indispensability, take the opportunity to improve your team's thinking about what is truly essential.

RESPONDING DIRECTLY TO EXPENSIVE SENTENCES

Try re-directing the conversation from a vague scarcity to specific discussion that connects to your goals.

❝ *No one is irreplaceable, even though I agree that Patrick has excellent skills in several important areas. I guess we won't know how hard it would be to replace those skills unless we scan the candidate pool résumés, and I admit I haven't done that in a few months. Have you?"*

❝ *Alfonse has contributed a ton to this team and it's hard to imagine letting him go. But to be a long-term fit on our team, he has to have the cultural values to go along with the subject expertise. Have we fully accounted for the cost of his behavior and attitudes on the team as a whole?*

❝ *I know that SuperCo has a great product, and perhaps there's no one else with it. But let's detail exactly how that translates to our business results and then consider other pathways."*

> ❝ *What is it that makes Sue indispensable? Is it her expertise? If so, how do we get that shared among the team? I'm nervous about anyone's being that irreplaceable, even me. Let's make sure we are documenting processes and sharing knowledge so we're not in a fix if Sue or anyone else wins the lottery."*

Group Conversation Topics

The following questions might be worth asking on your team, especially if you sense you are overly swayed by vendors, people, products, or technologies that "cannot be replaced":

Our beliefs about experts:

- What makes someone an expert?
- How much does an expert know about her field?
- What are the limits of one person's expertise?

Our beliefs about knowledge and expertise:

- Can expertise be acquired?
- Can it be documented? Should it be shared?
- Are we a learning organization?

Resources versus Results:

- Is our team focused on quantitative goals (results) more than on our actions or efforts (resources)?
- Which do we talk about more on our team: resources or results?
- What do we celebrate or compensate people for?
- What is more important on this particular project?

EXERCISES TO CREATE MORE OPTIONS AND REDUCE DEPENDENCE

. . . .

The specific tactics below can move your team from no options to many options.

EXERCISE: TRANSLATE RESOURCES INTO RESULTS

In many cases, the belief that a product, a technology, or even a person is irreplaceable is rooted in confusion between resources and results. Resources are the means to an end, and results are the ends themselves. Here are a few examples:

RESOURCE	RESULT
Accounting software	Timely, accurate reporting
Social media services	Greater awareness; more sales leads
Cleaning services	A clean, pleasant office

While we often pay for resources, what we really want is results. This confusion is muddied by vendors who often focus more on the products and services they sell than on the problems they solve for customers. (Ian Altman and I write about this at length in our book *Same Side Selling*.)

Our focus should always be on the results. Any time we get hung up on one particular product, feature, technology, or team, it's an indicator that we may be thinking about the resources more than the results. It may help to step back from the product, technology, or process and ask some high-level questions:

- What is the problem you are solving?

- What do great results look like?

The results should always be separated from the means of getting to the results. When there seems to be only one path to a goal, that goal is almost always being viewed too narrowly.

EXERCISE: IDENTIFY FACTORY INPUTS AND OUTPUTS

When you seem to be in a situation with an essential vendor or limited options, conduct the Factory exercise. Draw a factory on a whiteboard (add some smokestacks for fun), and leave space on the left and right for inputs and outputs, respectively.

What inputs are required? What outputs? If we applied this construct to the internet advertising story, for example, we might arrive at the following:

ADVERTISING BUDGET \$ + AD COPY (INPUTS) ▶ FACTORY ▶ QUALIFIED LEADS (OUTPUTS)

Then we could ask the question, what other "factory" will take our money and advertisements and turn them into leads? For another example, consider a fulfillment shipping vendor. In that case the factory equation might look like this:

PRODUCTS + ORDER DETAILS (INPUTS) ▶ FACTORY ▶ GOODS DELIVERED TO CUSTOMER (OUTPUTS)

Again we ask, is there any other way we can start with these inputs and end up with those outputs? What other path or means might get us to our desired results?

Sometimes this exercise might even raise questions of scope that lead to better solutions, such as: "Maybe we could find a vendor who could help us develop more effective ads," or "I wonder if a fulfillment company could take the warehousing off our hands?"

Exercise: Ask "How Might We...?"

"How might we" is a more conversational variant of the Factory exercise. It starts by shifting the focus from the "irreplaceable" resource to the result. That is, change "Bob knows the system like no one else" to "With Bob on the team, we are able to quickly diagnose any problem we have with the system."

Now consider the second half of that statement, and convert it to "How Might We". Brainstorm by asking the question "How might we quickly diagnose any problem we have with the system?"

This brainstorming process works best in a team setting, preferably with four to six people.

CHAPTER 8

"THE CUSTOMER IS ALWAYS RIGHT"

"We'll have to customize this for them."

"They have special requirements."

"If we don't do this for them, I think we'll lose this customer."

IN THE MOVIE *BRUCE ALMIGHTY*, DOWN-ON-HIS-LUCK BRUCE VOICES so much anger at life's unfairness that God grants him a stint running the universe (or at least that part of the universe near Buffalo, New York). Among the job duties of the newly almighty Bruce—played by Jim Carrey—is answering prayers. After he realizes that he can convert all incoming prayers into an email interface, Bruce sits down with some coffee to answer the million-plus requests, one at a time. The email subject lines state the nature of the prayers:

> *Good grades*
> *Safe trip*
> *I'm lonely*
> *Win the lottery*
> *Lost puppy*
> *Dad's surgery*
> *Boyfriend's job*

Bruce powers through thousands of requests for hours on end, only to realize that the quantity of requests is growing more quickly than he can respond. Hopelessly frustrated, he finds an "Answer All" button in the email program and types a global response to all of the email prayers: YES. With a satisfied smile, he leans back in his chair, relaxes, and sighs, "Now everybody's happy."

But it doesn't quite work out that way. The following scenes depict confusion and catastrophe throughout the city as individual requests collide into collective chaos and a melee of unintended consequences. (Among other things, an abundance of lottery winners reduces the prize to less than $20.) Bruce begins to see that maybe being God isn't as simple as he had thought. The scene poses a profound question: what if God answered everyone's prayer requests in exactly the way they asked?

We'll save the tough theology for another book, but each of us has an arena in which we field requests and answer to people. A question that we might have to answer is: what if I give people everything they ask of me? Or, what if the customer is always right?

"The customer is always right" is attributed to the retailer Marshall Field, who developed the first department stores in the 1880s in Chicago. At a time when the phrase "Buyer Beware" summed up how most people approached shopping, Field changed the landscape of retailing. His stores—which still bore his name until the early 2000s—were the first to use window displays, provide bridal registries, offer unconditional refunds, and implement many other innovations. Field set a new standard for service and was rewarded with many loyal customers.[24]

More recently, technology and media have brought greater visibility to customer service. Socially driven resources such as Yelp, Angie's List, and online product reviews drive billions of dollars in sales. Companies like Amazon and Nordstrom are widely praised for the way they make transactions easy and enjoyable for their customers, and their stock valuations reflect that approval.

In many ways, this is a golden age for the customer. It would seem that to succeed in the marketplace, anyone selling anything would have to listen carefully to what the customer asks for and tailor their offerings to match that desire. But business success is not a simple formula of listening and responding.

The Dangers of Following the Customer

Following the customer's preference might win the sale, and that sale might be exactly what we think we need. But when we act on the premise that customers are scarce and therefore each one must be catered to, we go down a road that often leads to financial losses and strategic blunders. It seems like a paradox, but those very customers who bathe us in adoring service ratings can drive us out of business if we are not thoughtful and deliberate in how we serve them.

That's not to say that customer love is a bad thing or that you can claw your way to the top over unhappy buyers. Since every business needs customers, the buyer's point of view certainly does matter. But it's critical to discern which buyers are right and how they are right.

Our "Customers" and Expertise

This Expensive Sentence is not limited to the buyer-seller relationship. The principles and pitfalls here apply far beyond traditional customer relationships. The buyer-seller dynamic provides a clear example because of the direct exchange of money for products or services.

The truth is that any outward-focused relationship is vulnerable to over-responsiveness. Have you known someone to get into trouble with one of these beliefs?

My friends are always right.

My family is always right.

Any of us who are mindful of others can fall out of balance in how we respond to others. This statement applies even when money is not part of the relationship. We will focus on the marketplace, but consider these other Expensive Sentences:

- **ARTIST:** The critic is always right.
- **TEACHERS:** The student is always right—or—The parents are always right.
- **PASTORS:** The churchgoer is always right.
- **PARENTS:** The child is always right—or—The child should always be happy.
- **COACHES:** The athlete is always right.
- **CEO:** The employee is always right.

The "always right" philosophy seems a poor fit for some of these relationships, and we can imagine the fallout that might ensue. For example, have you ever heard the medical expression, "The patient is always right"?

Imagine that you went in to see your family doctor and said, "Doc, my stomach's really hurting—I think you need to take my appendix out." The doctor would then reply, "Well, the patient is always right, so let's get you into surgery at once!" While we all have insights into our own health and we may know our own bodies well, it's outlandish to think that we could diagnose and practice medicine as well as a doctor with decades of training and experience. It's not that doctors are infallible—every doctor has biases and blind spots. But in the field of medicine, the customer (i.e., the patient) generally has no assumption of expertise. We go to doctors because they are the experts, and we know that.

In your field, do you know more about your subject matter than your customers do?

Most of my career has been spent in procurement: helping companies buy services and products. In many cases, companies use a Request for Proposal (RFP) to help them document their requirements and communicate with vendors. When I work with a company to create an RFP, we usually have a good idea of what we need. Then as we receive responses and talk to vendors, inevitably we learn more about the marketplace and the solutions. We often learn more about my client's company and problem because the vendors ask questions that we hadn't considered. These vendors have seen many companies in similar situations and have developed a much better understanding of the problem and solution than we have.

Reflecting on this experience, I see that when I have been in the role of customer, I have not always been right. In full candor, it would be more accurate to say that I've always been at least a little bit wrong.

It's not that customers are always wrong (any more than they are always right)—if someone is buying a gallon of milk or a container of rivets, he may know exactly what he wants up front. But if you are in the business of serving customers, it's worth reflecting on how often your customers know exactly what they need when they start talking to you.

THE COST OF CUSTOMERS BEING WRONG

Former Ohio State University football coach Woody Hayes is credited with first expressing a rather glum philosophy about the forward pass. By his reckoning only three things could happen when the quarterback threw the ball, and two of them were bad.[25] (The three outcomes being that the intended receiver could catch the ball—that's the good one—or the ball could fall to the ground [bad] or be intercepted by the other team [even worse!].)

Only three things can happen when you assume the customer is right. Again, two of them are negative:

- **STRATEGIC MISSTEPS.** Assuming the customer is right means that you will follow their lead. If this takes you away from your planned agenda or course, it can dilute your strategic focus or cause you to go in a direction that is less successful.

- **EXCESSIVE COST.** Fully responsive customer service is expensive. It means that special requests must be catered to. If your business model does not account for these costs and charge commensurate fees, meeting those customer requests can devour profits.

The positive third outcome is quite positive indeed: ecstatic customers and business success. To this point, we might observe that despite Hayes's warning every modern American football team relies on the forward pass. The three outcomes remain, but coaches and players have learned that the right throws in the right situations will lead to success. The same is true for pleasing the customer; it's hard to imagine that any company could be successful without high customer satisfaction. The key is responding to the customer in a way that advances strategy and contains cost. This is not always obvious, even for mature companies.

LEGO WITHOUT THE BRICKS?

Hundreds of millions of children grew up with Legos. The colorful, interlocking, plastic bricks have stimulated billions of hours of playtime as they have been fashioned into castles, trucks, dinosaurs, rockets, buildings, and anything else that can be imagined by a child. Lego is one of the few iconic world brands that is almost universally loved.

Lego has also been a successful business. During the twenty years after the Lego brick was patented in 1958, the company grew steadily to $180M in revenue. In the late 1970s, Lego introduced the mini-figure along with its castle and space themes, and for the next fifteen years, sales doubled every five years. And then growth stopped. In 1998, for the first time in its fifty-year history, the company lost money.

It appeared that Lego buyers were suddenly scarce. This crisis caused Lego to evaluate the marketplace and look for new ideas. One of the key steps they took was a market survey of children in its target customer group. What they found was surprising and—for Lego—somewhat disturbing: *most children they surveyed did not like construction toys.* The segments that were growing fastest in the toy market included video games, pre-assembled toys, and brands that tied directly to TV-show characters.

With an implicit belief that the customer was always right, Lego boldly adapted to these findings by launching several new product lines. These ventures included video games, toys that were nearly assembled right out of the box, and Lego TV shows with characters.

Did these responsive changes save Lego?

They did not. In fact, following the customer nearly killed the company. In 2003 Lego lost 300 million dollars and narrowly avoided bankruptcy. Few of the product lines were embraced by customers, and those that were often stole shelf space from other Lego products, cannibalizing existing product lines. The new products also doubled the number of Lego parts that needed to be manufactured, adding enormous production costs.

Thankfully—for those of us who love the bright little bricks—Lego was able to recover. They did so with a marked rejection of some of the "lessons" they had learned from their prior research. The company slashed the number of parts by over 30 percent and required that all new Lego sets be made from that core catalog. They discontinued numerous product lines that were less connected to building.

As one of the senior managers at Lego summed it up, "We had to stay with the play that we knew how to do." This strategy was not responsive to the customer's requests or the demands of the marketplace. Yet the customers responded, leading to record revenues and profitability to Lego.[26]

THREE AREAS WHERE CUSTOMERS ARE OFTEN MISTAKEN

If you don't like to label those who pay you with the attribute "wrong," it might be more useful to think of customers as being under-informed or lacking expertise. After all, customers might be experts on their problems, but it is highly doubtful that they would claim expertise on the solutions. They need you because you are the expert.

There are several specific ways in which customers can misunderstand who you are or how you can help them. Sometimes the misunderstanding is not even about you or your services; sometimes customers just don't know what they want or need, even when they think they do.

AREA 1: CUSTOMERS MISUNDERSTAND WHAT IS MOST IMPORTANT TO THEM

If you were shopping for a new gadget, would you be savvy enough to buy the gadget that would bring you the most satisfaction? Evidence suggests that the answer is no.

In 2006, the *Harvard Business Review* published an eye-opening study about the buying decisions of consumers. The study showed that when people were shopping, they were drawn to items with higher quantities of features. Consumers greatly preferred enhanced versions of products—coffee makers or washing machines with timers, smart TVs that connected to the internet directly, or cars with integrated GPS or entertainment systems—to their simpler counterparts. However, when customers were later surveyed about which products they were most satisfied with, their preferences went in the opposite direction. By a wide margin, customers were most satisfied with those products that had limited functionality.[27]

In other words, customers were almost universally mistaken about what was really important to them. When they saw it on the shelf, they thought that they wanted the Swiss Army Knife with sixteen attachments, but in practice, what they really used and valued was the simple two-blade version.

Customers don't always understand what will drive long term value. Depending on what you are selling and the nature of your customer relationships, it may be advisable to educate your customers so that they are more likely to have long-term satisfaction with their purchase.

Area 2: Customers Misunderstand the Relationship

There's a story about a businessman who hired Frank Lloyd Wright to build a house for him. He explained that when he hired the renowned architect he understood that Wright was working for him, but then his perspective shifted and it seemed like they were working together. Finally, he admitted, it became clear that he—the owner of the home—was working for Wright.[28]

The businessman's confession reveals the tradeoffs that may be part of working with a great artist. It also presents a spectrum of possible working relationships between a buyer and a seller.

In your customer relationships, who owns the vision? Are you implementing the customer's ideas, are you working together to develop the vision, or does the customer expect you to provide the direction?

When a buyer thinks she has bought one thing and the seller believes he has sold something else, friction can occur. Complex or longer-term purchases provide more opportunity for this type of misunderstanding.

Because different companies have different approaches, it is important for the seller to ensure that the buyer knows how the relationship will be structured. Is he buying muscle to execute, or brains to design, or a combination of both? How will decisions be made during the project?

AREA 3: CUSTOMERS MISUNDERSTAND YOUR BUSINESS MODEL

Imagine that you sit down for dinner at the nicest restaurant in town. You are seated and the server graciously meets you and asks if there are any food restrictions. You share that you are gluten-sensitive and lactose-intolerant and sucrose-belligerent (I just made that last one up, but by the time you are reading this, it may be a real thing). Your professional server smiles and says, "No problem! I'll speak to the chef and we will create something that delights your senses and meets your requirements."

Now imagine sharing the litany of your special needs at a fast-food hamburger shack. The befuddled teenager behind the counter says, "Um… maybe you should just get a cup of water?"

The high-end restaurant and the burger joint have very different models. Customers would be mistaken to expect similar experiences or levels of service and customization.

Companies that have not clearly defined their business models are more susceptible to customers with differing demands. If your model is to be highly responsive and accommodating to individual customers, you can position yourself in that market segment, but you will have a difficult time competing with vendors who are less responsive.

Individual customers should never change a provider's business model. While in some cases business models can change over time and may respond to the marketplace, it should not happen as a response to a specific customer's requests or demands.

Customized or Standardized

Several years ago I was helping a client choose between two firms offering competing services in outsourced financial operations. Though the companies were direct competitors, their respective business approaches were quite different.

Vendor A said: We'll work with your existing team and processes. We can use whatever accounting software you have; our team can offer as little as one person part-time, or we can assign a full team; and you can set the level of reporting you want.

Vendor B said: We will design a migration to our chosen accounting software – which is the only software we use. All of our clients get reports that look like this, and you'll get them on these three specified dates every month. Here's what your invoices will look like; here's the process for expense reports, etc.

In effect, *Vendor A* was saying, "You, Mr. Customer, are right. Whatever you want or need is just fine; we can accommodate you." *Vendor B* was saying, "This is our process. We know how to do it well in this way, and all of our customers need to conform."

Vendor A could be considered much more flexible and responsive, and *Vendor B* could be considered rigid or highly structured. There is not necessarily one right business design—either approach can be successful if the vendor is positioned to deliver it. What is almost certain to fail is an in-between approach that attempts to provide full flexibility *and* full structure, or an execution that simply follows whatever the most recent customer asks for.

The Right Customers Are Rarely Wrong

If you can't quite shake the notion that the customer is always right, maybe it will help to be more selective in defining who your customers are. Lego decided that children who did not want the creative building experience were not the customers that they were aiming to attract.

Do you know who your customers are? Have you defined them in terms of what they value?

Defining "Customer"—Five Guys Burgers and Fries

Given the growth of the Five Guys chain, there's a good chance you have seen the stores or tasted the burgers. Five Guys claims to be the most reviewed restaurant in the world. They have a menu consisting of hamburgers, hotdogs, and French fries. That's about it.

Years ago I took part in a meeting with Jerry Murrell, the CEO of Five Guys, and his first group of franchisees. Some franchisees in the group were pressing Murrell for changes in the stores' menu and pricing in response to customer feedback. Some wanted to add turkey sandwiches and milkshakes to the menu.

Murrell was unyielding. He saw no reason to change his approach. Five Guys was routinely named "the best burger in town" by newspapers and magazines and typically had the highest food ratings of any of its competitors. Murrell attributed that to his focus. He reasoned that it would weaken the brand to add anything to the menu that would not be universally perceived as the best in the world. "People have different tastes for milkshakes and turkey sandwiches. As soon as one reviewer doesn't love it, it means we are getting poor reviews for something that isn't even what we want them to eat." Five Guys was aiming to be the best restaurant for lovers of hamburgers. Turkey lovers could go elsewhere to satisfy their cravings.

The conversation became emotional when a franchisee pleaded to lower prices: "It costs over $10 to get a burger, fries, and a drink." Again, Murrell was not moved, and the way he responded struck me:

> "Sure, people complain about the prices. But not *customers*. Our customers are happy to pay because they know our burgers are worth it."

In other words, just because someone came into the store and bought a meal didn't make him a customer—at least not in Murrell's mind. A true Five Guys customer was someone who appreciated their offerings and enjoyed the full value.

If your customers are wrong, maybe it's because you need to redefine who your customers are.

Firing Your Customers

The idea of serving only a specific segment of customers is widely practiced. In fact, at some level it is part of every business. It starts implicitly in the sales process. Your pricing and product offerings attract some clients and repel others who either don't want what you have or don't value it enough to pay your prices.

If you are selling hamburgers or another relatively simple retail item, your process of choosing your customers may end at the point of sale. But when the relationship is longer and has more variables, a more sophisticated method may be required to determine who the right customers are. The answer can take the form of a customer profitability analysis.

Do you know how much profit your customers are generating? Who is your most profitable customer? Are there some customers who are causing you to lose money? Unfortunately, acting on the premise that the customer is always right often leads to unprofitable customers.

Moving forward with customers that generate losses is a path to bankruptcy, so when an unprofitable customer is discovered, action must be taken. Sometimes that means raising fees or rates to cover additional services. Sometimes it might mean conveying to the customers that their expectations should be different.

Sometimes the best answer is "goodbye." Most people find it challenging to part ways with a paying customer, but it is sometimes necessary. An evolving enterprise may outgrow a customer who isn't willing or able to change their expectations. It recalls the breakup line, "It's not you, it's me. I'm just a different person than I used to be."

THREE FALLACIES BEHIND OVER-RESPONSIVENESS

The beliefs behind the words get us in trouble. When you hear "they're asking for this, we better do it" or some other variant of this Expensive Sentence that overemphasizes responsiveness, it may be time to examine whether your team buys into one of the traps below.

FALLACY 1: REVENUE IS MORE IMPORTANT THAN PROFIT

The *Forbes* 500 list and the *Inc.* Fastest Growing list are based on company revenues. When a company is mentioned in the newspaper as a 3-billion-euro company or an 80-million-dollar company, those figures (again) refer to revenue. Salespeople are typically rewarded on total sales captured, as opposed to profits.

Our world is much more focused on revenue than on profit. Given this backdrop, and the fact that many people work in business without a solid understanding of finance, it is to be expected that most people in the workplace value revenue more than profits. A belief that customers are always right amplifies that revenue bias.

A classic scenario illustrates revenue bias: the salesperson, eager to close a big deal, presents a long list of requests from a prospect for customizations and accommodations. Management reluctantly approves the changes because the prospect is a "big fish" that would boost revenue. Then after a long sales process, the company gets the deal. However, after they fully account for all of the changes, they realize they are losing money on the customer. They have successfully grown the company in terms of revenue, but detracted from profitability.

FALLACY 2: ANY CUSTOMER IS A GOOD CUSTOMER

There are times when the most urgent need at a company is to bring in a sale. But even in those seasons, there are still some clients you will decline and some projects you will not want. Does your team understand the characteristics of your target customers?

This fallacy is closely related to the first, as nearly all good customers will be profitable customers. But at times the analysis will be more than financial, as when good customers share certain values or advance the company's strategy.

For example, imagine an electrical contracting company that has decided it is better positioned to serve commercial customers than residential customers. There may be easy sales available for residential customers, but if the company takes on that work they will not have the bandwidth to pursue and serve the commercial customers that will be the foundation for the future.

Fallacy 3: Customers Are More Important Than Employees

The idea that the customer comes first has been replaced in some companies with the concept of putting the employee first. Costco is among the most prominent companies that explicitly value employees above customers.

It's worth noting that Costco has excellent customer service. Many business leaders profess that if they take care of their employees well, the happy employees will then take far better care of the customers. Conversely, a worker who feels demeaned or undervalued by his boss may let those feelings spill into customer interactions.

The foundation of great service is to know your team's identity and strengths, and to communicate those well both inside and outside the organization. That knowledge provides the wisdom to make right decisions on whom to serve, what to do, and what to leave undone.

WISE REPLIES TO "THE CUSTOMER IS ALWAYS RIGHT"

. . . .

The best time to manage the damage of an Expensive Sentence is right after you hear it. The response scripts and conversation topics below can help your team find the right level of responsiveness to your customers.

RESPONDING DIRECTLY TO EXPENSIVE SENTENCES

When someone on your team suggests that the customer is always right, try one of the following responses:

❝ *We certainly want to provide excellent service, but we have to do that in a way that supports our strategy and economics. Does this client and its needs match up with what we can deliver consistently and profitably?"*

❝ *Sure, the customer is always right, but some customers might be right for one of our competitors. If they don't understand and appreciate our value proposition—or if they are just jerks—we can't succeed in making them happy."*

❝ *I love your focus on serving the customer, but for us to accommodate this one means that we won't be able to serve our other customers consistently and affordably."*

❝ *I agree that our customers are always right, but maybe we need to refine our understanding of who our target customer is. Beyond just the industry and size of the prospect, what are the values of our target customer? What is the organizational maturity? What are the specific circumstances in which we can deliver huge value and hit a home run?"*

TOPIC FOR DISCUSSION: WHAT KIND OF CUSTOMERS DO WE WANT?

This discussion is related to the profitability exercise below, but is more of a qualitative assessment to profile clients that match your team's strategy and culture. You may want to prepare for the conversation by sending out a survey to individuals throughout your team. Ask the following questions:

1. How would you describe our best customers today?

2. Roughly what percentage of our customers meet that description?

3. What should our best customers look like two years from now?

Compile the results and note the similarities and differences in the responses. Your team may need better communication about the types of clients you serve, or there may be agreement that certain customer relationships should be changed or gracefully ended.

EXERCISES TO FIND THE RIGHT CUSTOMERS

If your team needs more clarity on whom they are aiming to serve, the following exercises may add definition.

EXERCISE: BUILD AN EXPERTISE MAP

Do your clients understand where your expertise can help them? Does your team know where it adds the most value? To clarify, make an "expertise map" out of a simple table that identifies which parties hold the most proficiency in different areas.

An expertise map for a graphic design company might look something like this:

SUBJECT	OUR CUSTOMERS	EXTERNAL VENDORS	OUR COMPANY
Cutting edge design trends			✕
Graphic Design software			✕
Leading the Creative Process			✕
Website Design		✕	
Website look & feel	✕		
Clients' goals	✕		

If this type of expertise map is reviewed at the beginning of the project, it can avoid confusion about who will be doing what.

Sometimes it might even clear up a misunderstanding or spur an important conversation:

> "Oh, I thought that we would lead the creative process, but you guys like to do that?"

> "So you don't do website design? Is there someone you recommend for that?"

Areas where it's unclear who the expert is, or where both parties claim to have expertise can be trouble areas if they are not acknowledged and planned for.

EXERCISE: RANK CUSTOMER PROFITABILITY

Understanding customer profitability is essential to improving profitability and to ensuring the right kind of growth. Profitability analyses can include detailed cost and time accounting and be extremely sophisticated. Sometimes a thorough study is justified, but most companies can develop useful profitability rankings using only a few pieces of data. Here are some shortcut questions:

a. Which customers are hard to keep happy?

b. Which customers need custom support?

c. Which customers don't really understand our value?

Your customer support team will have good instincts as to which customers are least profitable, but be sure to bolster the instincts with data: trouble tickets, custom requests, complaints, time spent supporting, etc.

When that data is assembled and viewed in light of customer revenue, you will be close to a good understanding of customer profitability. At a minimum, you will be able to perform a triage and classify customers as 1) definitely profitable, 2) not sure, and 3) unprofitable.

CHAPTER 9

"WE CAN PROBABLY DO THAT OURSELVES"

"Why should we pay someone else to do that?"

*"We did that at our old company;
I think I can figure it out."*

*"If you want something done right, you have to
do it yourself."*

"We can handle that in-house."

Have you ever leapt into a home improvement project with enthusiasm, only to realize—many hours and frustrations later—that the job demanded more than you had expected? Or maybe you've heard a friend share a story that ended in a sentence like one of these:

"After the third try, we decided to call in a real electrician."

"It was then that I vowed never to work with cement again."

"So I guess we saved money… if my time is worth three dollars an hour."

"Eighteen months later, we hired professional painters to finish the job."

Most veteran homeowners have learned the hard way that there are some jobs beyond their capacity. They may take on some projects that match their time, interests, and skill levels, but they also know when to call in professionals.

In the workplace, every team faces questions of what to do itself and when to hire help. It's one of the few decisions in business that cannot be avoided; even a team that aims to outsource everything cannot out-source the outsourcing. Build-or-buy decisions collectively shape the day, the team, and the company as they apply at multiple levels:

- The functional level—What do we outsource, and what do we take on with our existing staff? Where might we need to hire more people?

- The team level—What should our group do, and what should we leave to other groups in our organization? What's our job, and where are the limits?

- The individual level – What is my role? What should I take on, and when should I tactfully say no? How should I focus my time and effort?

Drawing the boundaries between what is inside and what is outside is a vital skill; and like other skills, it can be improved. When we get these answers right, we avoid taking on too much or taking on the wrong tasks. But it's not always a simple analysis.

Most teams are prone to undervalue their time, overestimate their abilities, and underappreciate the availability of services and expertise in the marketplace. Each of these tendencies tips the scale toward doing more in-house, whether or not that's actually the best decision.

The wrong answers can lead to the corporate version of the Do-It-Yourself disaster:

- You let the tech support team take on account management, and learned that they didn't have the suitable customer relationship skills.

- Your AP clerk stepped into customer billing and left behind a financial tangle that took your accountant months to straighten out.

- An eager marketing analyst agreed to build a new web page, but after four months had barely gotten started.

We think of "yes" as a positive word, but when your team accepts a project that would be better left to someone else, it may end up increase risk, lower quality, and cause delays. It may not even save money, though the hope of saving money is often the primary reason to do something ourselves.

WHY TRYING TO SAVE MONEY CAN COST YOU MONEY

Saving money can be costly. Let's unpack this irony in the context of build-or-buy. Completing a do-it-yourself project, whether at home or at the office, means that the dollars you would have otherwise paid outside professionals can stay in your wallet. That's good.

But of course, the project will take time to complete—either your time or that of someone on your team. Time is a real cost that is often both undervalued (putting a low value on your time) and underestimated (thinking a job will take less time than it actually does).

Let's consider some less obvious components of the cost of doing things ourselves:

- **The cost of doing the job right.** On top of the supplies required for the job, there may be specialized tools needed or additional time invested to learn proper technique.

- **The cost of doing the job wrong.** If the task is done incorrectly, there may be cleanup costs—in some cases paid to those very professionals that you had intended to avoid.

- **The cost of delay.** Part of the value of having an outside specialist work on your project is having the luxury of holding someone else to deadlines. When you are finding hours for a project while keeping on with your real job, it's harder to expect the same priority or enforce the same accountability.

- **The cost of risk.** When the right vendors are hired, they take the work off your plate—and they also take the worry. They are the experts and they will ensure the results. Even when you can get the job done yourself, the quality of your end product might be different from what a true professional would have delivered.

It's important to note that these costs can arise even if you do hire professional help, because sometimes "professional" is less professional than we would like. (If you find four people that have hired contractors to complete home renovations, three of them may have horror stories about the costs above or something worse.) But in most cases where specialty professionals are available, getting the right help will reduce costs.

The do-it-yourself project gone wrong may fizzle out or end in a spectacular explosion—sometimes literally. In either case, the costs of saying "we can do that ourselves" become clear in the aftermath. You clean up the mess, pay for the fix, and move on with more wisdom for the next decision.

If the painful lessons of a DIY-gone-wrong help you stick more closely to your core skills, then the education may be a great value.

Because, as we will see, the price can be even higher when the job goes right.

THE TRAP OF SUCCESS: INVISIBLE OPPORTUNITY COSTS

Unfortunately, failing at a task when we do it ourselves is not the only concern. Far greater damage can ensue when the project actually goes smoothly. The near-term win might feel good, but it could also seduce you down a path of hidden costs and confused strategies.

This apparent paradox relates to opportunity costs. Opportunity costs kick in when secondary activities distract from a company's core: the functions that it does best, that it gets paid for, and that advance its mission.

The following simple illustration might be useful to share with your team (I include it because I have learned that many people can benefit from a practical illustration of opportunity cost):

Imagine a doctor who resists hiring an office manager because she doesn't want to pay the salary. Then she spends half of her time scheduling appointments and handling paperwork and has to reject patients. Is that doctor saving money by not hiring the office manager? From a pure cash perspective, the doctor is in fact saving money. She doesn't have to pay an additional salary. Yet our instincts tell us that she is making a poor financial decision.

It's wrong to simply look at the doctor's cash outflow because that is ignoring the opportunity cost. The right decision requires that we consider how much more revenue the doctor could generate by doubling her available time for patient appointments. In all likelihood, that income would more than cover the cost of a qualified office manager.

To put it another way, the greatest cost of saying "we can do that ourselves" is likely to be neither money nor risk, but time and energy diverted from more important work. Every non-core task your team accepts brings a cost in opportunity. If the marketing team decides to do the technical project of building a website, then every minute they are coding, designing, and testing is time that they are not spending on marketing.

Steve Jobs famously proclaimed that "Strategy is about saying no." This simple maxim reflects a deep understanding that any new project has the potential to dilute focus and distract a team from its primary goals. It is rare that any team can pursue several diverse activities and achieve excellence in all of them.

WHY WE THINK WE CAN DO IT OURSELVES

It's not just the worthy desire to save money that leads us to do things we shouldn't. If it seems like "we can probably do that ourselves" is leading your team to a course that isn't supported by strategy or economics, it may be rooted in one of the following less worthy motives:

- **Individual preference or promotion** — A teammate may take on a task because it's highly visible, because it would be a good learning experience, because it sounds fun, or because he doesn't have enough to do in his role. For some jobs, those reasons may be enough, but a strategic project requires a stronger rationale.

- **The lure of bright, shiny objects** — Years ago, the senior management of my company spent a substantial amount of time planning to build a customer service center in India. The center would have been useful to us, but it had nothing to do with our core business. As a company we wanted that service and thought, "We can probably do that ourselves." Thank goodness, the project never took off. But the fact that we spent many hours thinking and talking about it is alarming in itself. What were we thinking? A new, exotic project outside of our regular routines and expertise can be highly appealing. We are more vulnerable to this pull when our primary business feels like a grind or when we may be avoiding an unpleasant reality that we should be attending to.

- **Bias toward our own strengths** — It is said that if you only have a hammer, sooner or later every problem starts looking like a nail. Most of us are prone to overvalue our own strengths and perspectives. This tendency becomes a problem if bias toward our own abilities leads us to the wrong solution for a problem.

- **Fear of delegation** — Stubborn pride, ignorance, or small-mindedness can lead people to think that only they can do a certain task in the right way. (See more about the benefits of delegation back in *Chapter 2*.)

"IF YOU WANT SOMETHING DONE RIGHT, YOU HAVE TO DO IT YOURSELF"

This book examines a number of well-known proverbs and sayings. Most have an element of truth along with the potential to be misapplied. So I criticize old sayings with a measure of respect… usually. But the phrase "If you want something done right, you have to do it yourself" is utter nonsense and should always be challenged.

Thankfully, I often hear this sentence used in a teasing manner (as in, "Nice job trying to tell that story, Larry, but I'll take it from here. *If you want something done right…*"). But imagine what this implies if someone is not joking. What a pitiful worldview to think that only you can meet your standards. The arrogance and the loneliness! If you catch yourself thinking this Expensive Sentence, take a step back and get over yourself.

Decades ago, some industrial companies were known for a "not made here" mentality, in which innovations from outside the walls of the organization would be quickly dismissed. Today that line of thinking is outdated and naïve, given the abundance of innovation from all over the world. No one has a monopoly on the right way to do things, and those who insist on doing everything themselves will be left in the past.

For any given question or problem, we probably don't have the best answer. *This is good news.* The world holds an abundance of solutions and experts that can help us, if we let them.

SIZING UP THE TRUST FACTOR

Over the years, I have advised clients to outsource their IT or accounting departments. Numerous companies provide these services and generally offer lower costs and less risk to their clients. Despite these advantages, many company leaders resist hiring an outsourced firm out of concerns about trust. For something as important as data security or financial operations, they are not quite comfortable placing their trust in an outside company.

The emphasis on trust makes sense, but the assumptions behind it may be misguided.

When a company handles IT or accounting in-house, it puts its trust in the people who lead those departments, and in any subordinates who have access and privileges. The company trusts that team in character and in competence. In other words, the team must not only steer clear of fraud and carelessness, but must also keep up to date with current technology, processes, and policies.

An outsourced partner would have additional reasons to meet an even higher threshold of trust. First, consider the scale and scope of their business. While your internal team works for your company, a high-quality vendor serves a variety of clients with different needs. Serving many companies exposes the company to best practices and industry trends. It requires that they establish reliable practices, and gives them many repetitions of the most important tasks.

Second, think about the priority and importance of doing the function correctly. Since the outsourcer's sole purpose is to provide one area of service, a failure in that service would be catastrophic and could threaten the company's survival. To illustrate: if a landscaping company has an accounting problem, it's an accounting problem. If an accounting company can't get its books straight, it may signal that they are in the wrong business.

We are inclined to trust those around us because we know them. But if we look at the incentives to perform well and the consequences of failure, it often makes more sense to trust those outside our organization with specific tasks.

Too Important to Do Yourself

Payroll management is a striking example of outsourcing. Before outsourced payroll became commonplace, it may have seemed rather strange—if not reckless—to engage another company to handle employee compensation. Imagine how the owner of a mid-sized company might have reacted to a payroll service salesperson in the 1950s:

Sure, I can let someone else deliver our products. But now you want me to give our money to an outside company, and trust THEM to pay our people? What's more important than our money and our people?

Yet in the twenty-first century, virtually every company in the United States uses a third-party vendor to handle payroll. It's not uncommon for firms to set this up by phone or online, without even meeting anyone from the payroll company in person.

Payroll is a vital function and must be done correctly (that is, a company cannot mess up its payroll for long and continue to stay in business). Payroll has become a no-brainer to outsource.

At first glance, the previous two sentences may appear to be contradictory. But the reality is that the essential nature of payroll is the very reason that nearly every company chooses to outsource it. While our first instinct may be that certain tasks are "too important to let someone else do them," it may serve us better in today's marketplace to give the most critical tasks to someone else. There's a good chance that an outside specialist will be more reliable, affordable, and effective.

Increasing Access to Experts

Let's say I'm a car guy, and I like to do my own maintenance. Three times a year, I change the oil in my car. So that means that over ten years, I will perform thirty oil changes. I'll probably get competent at the task and be relatively efficient (at least by weekend gearhead standards). But compare that to a professional oil change shop. A technician there may perform thirty oil changes in a day. Next to his experience, mine becomes insignificant.

Perhaps when it comes to changing oil, the stakes are low enough and the task is simple enough that the difference in experience doesn't make a great deal of difference. (Then again, maybe it would.) But the principle applies to nearly every task in every field.

Yes, you could build your own company website, but would you rather figure it out on the job or trust a company that has built 100 websites? Sure, you can do your own public relations, but you may get better results with the help of someone who has twenty years of PR experience. Of course you can conduct your own vendor negotiations—it's not brain surgery, after all—but maybe someone who has negotiated with hundreds of vendors in the past decade would see a few angles you might not, and that might lead to bigger savings or better quality.

In the last century, the trend toward improved skill at specific tasks has accelerated as technology, mobilization, and communications have rapidly progressed. As a result, there are more opportunities to outsource today than there ever have been before. The internet and the global-shipping economy have given wider access to broader markets, meaning even more opportunity for specialization.

Think of this from the merchant's perspective: If one's calling was to make dachshund sweaters in the 1960s, the potential buyers would probably be limited to the village or city that he lived in. If only one in one hundred people owned a dachshund, and only 10 percent of those opted to clothe the sausage-shaped pets, the market would be rather small. Now in the age of the internet, the canine clothier can advertise quite efficiently around the world and deliver his products overnight. That's good for him, and also good for his customers: it means more sales, more scale, more expertise, and lower cost.

THE FREEDOM TO FOCUS

Nearly every question your organization can face has been confronted by dozens, hundreds, or thousands of teams before you. The convergence of specialization, globalization, and technology means that you probably have access to the answers. It is rare that you will be plowing completely new ground, and there may be very efficient solutions to your needs.

There may have been a time in which your first instinct should have been "we can probably do this ourselves." Perhaps there is still a place where that is true—maybe if you're stranded on a desert island or camping in isolation. If you are not in one of those remote scenarios and you need something done, the best first question is: Who can do this for us?

In many fields, not only are options increasing, but quality is improving as cost is decreasing. Understanding this movement is essential to having the right mindset when you're deciding when to build and when to buy.

If a management team chooses to outsource product development, marketing, shipping, customer service, and financial operations, numerous skilled vendors are waiting to take on that work. As mentioned earlier in this chapter, one of the only skills that the business leader absolutely must possess is the skill of deciding what to build with full-time employees versus what to buy from outside companies.

MAKING THE BUILD-OR-BUY DECISION

We've reviewed the potential costs of doing too much in-house, the reasons we lean toward self-reliance, and the ways that the marketplace has changed to offer more and better solutions than ever before. Maybe this has all seemed to point in one direction, but my intention has been to level the ground so that we can approach a build-or-buy decision with our eyes and our minds open.

The starting point is the activity in question. Whether you're mending a fence, launching a new product line, writing a white paper, or buying a company, you'll need to address a few simple questions before taking it on or looking for help. You'll need to assess your team's abilities, the financial costs of the project in question, and your team's schedules, and assess opportunity costs and agency costs.

QUALITY—CAN YOU DO THE JOB?

The first question prompted by the sentence "We can probably do that ourselves" is: Can you? Clearly, your team should not take on any job that it cannot perform to an acceptable standard. But how do you define what level of quality is good enough?

Consider two baselines. The first is the minimum performance required to meet the basic results you need. So if the task at hand was sending out a marketing newsletter, the question of quality would be first addressed by answering whether your team could write the content of the newsletter, format it acceptably, and then deliver it by mail or email to the target audience.

Assuming your team can meet the first baseline, the next baseline is a commercial standard. If you were to hire a PR firm to write and send out the newsletter, what would it look like?

Now considering both baselines, what is the difference? Is there a meaningful gap between your performance and that of the third party? Does that gap impact your results?

COST—HOW MUCH WOULD IT COST TO DO THE JOB?

If you conclude that you can do a job in-house and do it well enough, the next question is: what would it take? How much would it cost to do it in house?

The key comparison point is the cost to hire someone else to do the job. If you did hire a vendor, would the cost be greater than if you did the work yourself?

For small projects, it may be enough to perform a cursory "guess-timate" of costs both internally and with a vendor. (Just remember that a guesstimate is a guess; the only way to know the cost of an outside vendor is to get a price in writing.)

TIME—WHEN CAN YOU DO THE JOB?

If clear-eyed answers to the questions of quality and cost point to doing the job yourself, the next concern is the calendar. Can you do the job yourself in an acceptable timeframe without detracting from other important activities?

Time constraints are a valid reason to hire an outsider. If they are truly the only drivers—meaning you have the expertise to achieve the right quality and to do so at a good cost—then you are in a position of being limited purely by capacity. In that case, you can weigh the options of hiring a vendor to do the project versus hiring additional staff to add bandwidth.

MEASURING OPPORTUNITY COSTS

In any business, and even on a personal level, it is helpful to be able to calculate the financial opportunity cost of doing a given task or project. Doing this requires that you assign specific values to your time and the time of those on your team.

Varying Opportunity Costs

Opportunity costs are not absolute, but are related to the value of how time would be used, so they will be different for different roles on your team. If your software engineer has a backlog of high-impact projects, and the customer support team is idle 30 percent of the day, then the opportunity cost will be greater for the developer and it may be close to zero for the customer support team (until their schedule fills up).

Opportunity costs may vary seasonally, or even by the time of the day. If your company conducts a major conference in October, staff may be intensely busy in September. So while you might have taken on a project in-house at a different time of the year, the opportunity cost in September would be higher.

Yet another variable in calculating opportunity costs relates to focus and skill. Just because someone has 30 percent of her time free doesn't necessarily mean that she could take on a large project without its detracting from the other 70 percent.

All of these qualifiers suggest that calculating opportunity cost will not be an absolute indicator of whether to build or buy, but don't let that deter you from assigning a specific value to your time and running the numbers. Even estimates can be helpful in improving a decision.

A Personal Weekend Rate

When it comes to projects at home, opportunity costs are just as real. If you decide to build the patio yourself, that job will cut into weekend hours that may have been spent golfing with friends, going to kids' soccer games, or simply relaxing.

It can be useful to have a handy "weekend hourly rate" for yourself to use with decisions about home and lawn projects that you could either handle or hand off. If I call mowing the lawn a two-hour job and value my weekend time at $20 per hour, then it's simple math to see that paying a neighborhood teen $30 to do it for me is a win.

Then again, the project may be personally rewarding and a valued activity in itself. Or it may be something that I value doing with a friend or family member. In that case, I might waive my "fee" and give the project priority.

MEASURING AGENCY COSTS

Outsourcing a function rarely means you get to "toss it over the fence" and no longer pay it any attention. If you hire a vendor, there are costs associated with managing that vendor.

The costs of working through a third party like a vendor or broker are called *agency costs*. Agency costs include the cost of communication, the loss of control, the potential added risk in having an outside entity involved, and other administrative costs incurred when you don't do something yourself.

Economic scholars propose that agency costs are constant whether the agency is internal (on your team) or external (a vendor or contractor). In other words, the hassle and expense involved in managing a vendor should be no more than the effort required to manage an employee or internal team.

That's theory; in the real world agency costs may be higher with an outsourced vendor, or they may be lower. The cost depends somewhat on your own organization and on the vendor, on how well you communicate, and on the complexity of the service in question.

While there is no set formula to reliably predict agency costs, those costs are likely to be higher where there are fewer marketplace options and when the function is less mature. Conversely, agency costs will probably be lower where the market offerings are mature and plentiful (think payroll processing again, with millions of payrolls processed every month by outsourced providers).

To estimate agency costs, start by asking two questions:

- How hard is it to find a qualified vendor?

- How hard would it be to switch vendors if we had to?

When it's relatively easy to find and change vendors, it is likely that agency costs will be low. (It also means that it would be easier to find someone else to work with if you needed to.)

If you have worked through the basics of quality, time, and cost, and then considered the opportunity cost and agency costs, you'll have the information to make an informed decision.

STRATEGY IS THE SUM OF MANY SMALL DECISIONS

The build-or-buy decisions that are made from day to day and week to week are more than tactical. In practice, operations and strategy cannot be separated. When you decide to print your own annual reports, you are—to a small degree—getting in the business of printing. At one level, you are essentially competing against FedEx and other printers. It's not that you are trying to steal FedEx's customers (except for your own company), but you are betting that you can do that task as efficiently as they can.

The same principle applies if you decide to buy your own building instead of renting space, and then sublet some of your building to other companies. You are then entering the commercial real estate business. If you have several recruiters on staff, you are in the recruiting business.

There are times when the right decision is to print your own reports, buy the building, or hire a full-time recruiter. But when someone on your team says, "We can probably do that ourselves," it's fair to respond with strategic questions:

- Do we want to be in that business?

- Can we compete with the leaders in the field?

- Can we hire the best people in that industry?

KNOWING WHEN TO SAY NO

Is your team skilled in saying yes to the right things and saying no to the wrong things? Do you have criteria in place to evaluate what belongs in the core and what doesn't? Your team was built for a purpose, and that purpose informs what it should be doing.

Imagine that you are the CEO at Big Signs, Inc., a company that builds large outdoor signs for businesses, and that I work for you as the VP of sales. I've presented a case showing that we need a better way for the sales team to track their efforts, and I persuade you to invest in a sales tracking system. I believe that I know just how to build that system and that if I contract with a software team for six months, they can put it together under my direction.

You would be well within your rights—and quite wise—to ask if I had a background in software development, and to remind me that my job was getting more production out of our salespeople, not building systems. A better path would almost certainly be to buy an existing sales tracking system or, if necessary, to have one customized by a firm that specializes in that work. Even though selling may be my primary job, building sales tracking systems is probably not part of my core; it is not something that I'm regularly paid to do.

Now imagine that the company needs a sign to put in front of its new street-front location. Aha! Here we have a need which hits squarely at our core. Since other people pay us to create big signs, we can make our own and probably do it as efficiently as anyone else could. (At least we better be able to… and that sign better look *great*.)

There are numerous compasses that can help you find the true north of your core as an individual or a company. Without taking away from other approaches, I'll submit that the marketplace is a simple proxy. If a client buys a service from my company, that is proof that the service can be sold. It means we are professionals in that service.

"You guys can do that, can't you?"

Just because someone's willing to pay you doesn't always mean that you should say yes. Imagine a residential construction practice that specializes in finishing basements. One day the company president is finishing a project for a delighted client, who stops to admire the work. He says to the contractor: "we're thinking of putting a new deck on out back. You guys can do that for us, can't you?"

This type of affirmation and sales opportunity can become an Expensive Sentence if it leads us into a business that we don't want to perform. It would seem that a contractor with the expertise to finish a basement – with the electrical, plumbing, carpentry, and finishing capability – would also be skilled in building a deck, which seems relatively simpler. But maybe there are components of the job that are different and critical: such as moving earth and setting foundations. Perhaps the municipal permits and the potential weather constraints related to outdoor projects add complexity and cost.

While the new deck might be a project the contractor could do well, it may not fit into his business structure and plans. On the other hand, it could be a great opportunity to expand his business strategically. The point is that saying yes to paid work is a good thing when it aligns with deliberate strategy.

Different Paths of Growth: RCA versus GE

Have you seen the old picture of the dog listening to the antique record player?

That record player was made by RCA, which was a leader in the early decades of personal entertainment devices. It later achieved great success as the first mass distributor of electronic televisions. From this commanding and profitable position in consumer electronics, the company began asking the question "What else should we do ourselves?" They started investing in other areas. Throughout the 1960s and '70s, RCA became a wide-ranging conglomerate, acquiring companies in many diverse fields, from rental cars and frozen foods to book publishing and real estate. All of their purchases had merit individually, but they had little or nothing to do with making consumer electronics. While the management of RCA was tending to mergers and learning about new industries, several Japanese manufacturers introduced new advances on the television. They offered equal or superior products with lower pricing and subsequently took major market share from RCA. Finally, RCA tried to return to its core, but they did not succeed in getting back to the top of the television market. The value of the company tumbled, and in the mid-80s RCA was acquired.[29]

The collapse of RCA is considered an epic failure in American business, but it is not one of a kind. There are thousands of stories of companies large and small expanding too far and then paying the price for a lack of focus. (Maybe even a company you have worked for?)

What is especially interesting about the RCA story is the contrast between its history and the better-known story of the company which bought it. General Electric was also a diverse corporation with many unrelated business lines; however, its past shows that diversity does not necessarily lead to weakness or mediocrity.

Jack Welch became CEO of General Electric in 1981, after twenty years with the company as an engineer, manager, and vice president. He had experience in several different lines of business, and he saw that there was mediocrity in many areas of GE that hurt the company's reputation. At that time—when GE owned literally hundreds of product lines—could it trim back to just two or three? Realistically, this kind of downscaling was not viable. However, Welch took a different tack in pursuing excellence by ordering a systematic review and overhaul of the entire company.

How did Welch and GE answer the question of "should we be in this business?" The criterion was simple: GE had to be either first or second in the world in market share in every business that it preserved. Any product line for which they already held those positions was one they would keep. If GE had a business area that wasn't either leading or second in its respective industry, the company would fix it, sell it, or shut it down.

This approach of "number one, number two, or not at all" proved extremely successful for GE. Despite divesting itself of many lines of business, the company consistently posted record revenues and profits and increased its stock value forty-fold during Welch's CEO tenure.

Wise Replies to "We can probably do that ourselves"

. . . .

Does your team know where to draw the boundaries of its activity, at both the tactical and strategic level? This section contains specific tactics, exercises, and conversational text that can be used to break out of scarcity and find more options.

Responding Directly to Expensive Sentences

The starting point is language. Fight Expensive Sentences with better sentences. When someone suggests that you should take on tasks in-house that might be better handled by vendors, try customizing one of the following replies:

❝ *That's true, we could probably do that ourselves, and I don't doubt that we could do it well. But given our priorities and the fact that others are also providing that service, it's probably wiser to find a partner to do it."*

❝ *Does that fit into our strategic plan? I would hate to pull resources from our core efforts unless you see this as something that we are planning to take to market and sell in the next 18 months."*

❝ *Would anyone pay us to do that? I wonder if there are some complexities that we aren't seeing right now."*

❝ *I know your team could do this, and I don't doubt they could do it well, but I don't want to dilute their focus."*

GROUP CONVERSATION TOPICS

If the language of scarcity shows up frequently in your team's conversations, it may be helpful use the following diagnostic questions to work through several related beliefs.

Priority

- Do we know what our priorities are?
- Do we have enough resources?
- Is it possible we are trying to do too much?

Vendors and Partners

- Why do we use outside vendors?
- When do we use vendors versus doing things in-house?
- What have been our best experiences with an outside provider?

Core Activities

- What are the things we do best as a company?
- Are we trying to do things that are not in our core?
- What activities do we do in-house that no one would ever pay us for?

You can find free spreadsheets and templates for these exercises, as well as additional tactics to reduce scarcity, at *www.ExpensiveSentences. com.*

HOW TO HANDLE ANY EXPENSIVE SENTENCE

WELCOME TO THE FIGHT AGAINST EXPENSIVE SENTENCES. WE NEED you on the team, but maybe I should have started with a warning: awareness can be a burden, and you just might start hearing Expensive Sentences everywhere.

To prepare for the onslaught, we'll note a few sentences here that didn't get a chapter but may rear their heads in your neighborhood in the near future. Better still, we'll present a general approach to take on any Expensive Sentence with tact and effectiveness. Finally, we'll connect Expensive Sentences to some other concepts and lines of thinking that you may have come across, or that you may want to explore further.

A FEW MORE SENTENCES THAT ARE OFTEN COSTLY

In this book we have examined nine specific sentences in depth. Each of the nine has cousins with different wordings, and between them all we've covered much of the toxic wisdom and misleading language that degrades team decisions. But we didn't get them all. Here are a few more that are worthy of dishonorable mention:

"It's already under budget, so we don't need to negotiate."

Budgets are arbitrary and have little or no relation to the marketplace or value. If you've come in under last year's budget, but the market pricing has dropped 50%, then you are overpaying greatly. (If you wonder how the US government built up twenty trillion dollars of debt, one of the keys is budget-driven buying.)

"Great service is worth paying for."

Great service is nice, but sometimes you can get great service without paying more. In addition, service is a feature that may or may not get you closer to your business goals. If the service is not just good but unusual, and if it translates directly to your business success, then it may be worth paying for.

"These prices won't last."

Sales come and go; prices rise and fall. It's possible that you may miss out on a deal sometimes, but letting someone else's promotion schedule determine your purchasing decisions is a sure path to overpaying. This combination of scarcity and urgency leads to the wrong purchase, the wrong quantity, and the wrong price.

"It was on sale."

When my mom and dad got married—so the legend goes—my grandfather pulled aside his new son-in-law and offered a wry congratulatory warning. "Now she can start saving you money," he began. "I can't afford to have her save me any more money."

For the record, my mother has been frugal and wise in her spending as long as I have known her. But all of us are tempted to spend under the pretense of saving by many would-be Expensive Sentences:

- "It's a Groupon."

- "It was buy-one-get-one-free."

- "I had a 40% off coupon that was about to expire, so I couldn't resist."

These discounts can be valuable tools when used with discretion for planned purchases. But if the answer to "would I make this purchase without the discount?" is negative, you may be wiser to skip the deal and stick to your shopping list.

THREE QUESTIONS TO RE-WRITE AN EXPENSIVE SENTENCE

In the next week, you are likely to hear many potentially Expensive Sentences. You may even utter one yourself. When that happens, I hope you will respond with a simple reflection:

"Was that an Expensive Sentence?"

A sentence is just a sentence: it's not a person, it's not a company, and it's not necessarily a deep belief or even a fully-formed idea. We all are entitled to string together some clumsy or confusing words on occasion. If we gently challenge ourselves and others in real-time, we have the opportunity to improve our course quickly with little added cost. My hope is that you will adopt the conversational habit of evaluating sentences on your team and with your friends and family. The paragraphs below present a template to do just that.

Earlier we reviewed an alliterated list to help recognize the sentences: Stuck, Special, Scarce. More pointedly, we ask the three questions:

- Are you Stuck?
- Is someone Special?
- Is something Scarce?

When one or more of those answers indicates an Expensive Sentence, we can often defeat it with another set of three questions starting with Why, When, and What if:

1. Why is the Expensive Sentence true?
2. When is the Expensive Sentence true?
3. What if the Expensive Sentence is *not* true?

These questions form conversational arc from the first to the third. In that conversation we engage with the other person and build rapport, we examine our thinking together, and then we aim to enlighten them with a new perspective.

Engage: Why is the Expensive Sentence true?

The first question is asked in a spirit of humble enquiry. We're assuming that there is some validity to the sentence, for two reasons. First, as we've seen there is almost always some kernel of truth within every Expensive Sentence. Secondly, if our goal is to persuade someone to change their perspective, we are likely to be more successful by coming alongside and affirming their thinking rather than quickly shooting them down. (That is, we'll get better results with "That's interesting, let me think about that with you" than by declaring "What a block-headed thing to say.")

Remember that an Expensive Sentence is not inherently bad or stupid. In some cases, it may reflect true wisdom, and the goal of the first question is to identify why the sentence would be helpful in those cases. After we've established that there is some validity in the sentence (and hopefully built some rapport and increased trust along the way) we can ask the second question.

EXAMINE: WHEN IS THE SENTENCE TRUE?

The underlying premise of this second question is that there are some conditions that need to be present for the sentence to apply. Of course, the question also implies the converse, raising the specter that this might be one of those scenarios in which the sentence does not fit. From defining when the sentence applies in general, you can pivot to the specifics at hand:

> OK, so we've talked about how this sentence sometimes is true and at other times isn't. Are we sure this is one of those times where it applies? Why would it be? Why might it not apply here? How much confidence do we have either way?

The goal of the second question is to examine whether the general truths of the sentence match the particulars of this case. Any answer other than an airtight, categorical "YES" suggests that it's worth moving on to the third question.

ENLIGHTEN: WHAT IF THE SENTENCE IS NOT TRUE?

By raising some doubt about the sentence, we have given reason for hope. Maybe we're not stuck… maybe that vendor is not special in a way that limits our options or costs us money… maybe that something is not as scarce as we had thought. This is good news, and the point of asking "What if the sentence is not true?" is to identify specific possibilities that may be open to us now that our thinking is more free.

> "If they're not the only one in town that can do that project for us, there's a good chance we can find a better price and invest the difference in hiring a new teammate."

> "If we don't have to get the project started by next week, we can take some more time to find a better solution that might reduce our workload."

> "If he's not necessarily the only guy for me, then I guess I can raise my standards and start looking for Mr. Right."

I love the word *enlighten* for this third question because when we free someone from an Expensive Sentence, we are in fact bringing more light into their circumstances and also lightening their burden. Rewriting Expensive Sentences can truly change lives.

FITTING INTO A BIGGER PICTURE

As I shared in the introduction, I stumbled upon Expensive Sentences in the workplace. My lens initially was making corporate buying decisions, but soon widened in scope to include nearly all team decisions. I believe the label "Expensive Sentence" is a useful and novel term for these situations. But I cannot claim that this concept sprang fully formed from my brain; it connects with other recent and classic perspectives on how humans think and interact. I thought it might be helpful to make a few connections to those ideas.

SHAKESPEARE, THE BIBLE, AND SCIENCE

In the second act of *Hamlet*, the rhythmically-named duo of Rosencrantz and Guildenstern visit their old schoolmate who seems depressed. The Dane's melancholy surfaces when Hamlet refers to Denmark as a prison. His friends are puzzled – Denmark, a prison? They object, "We think not so, my Lord."

> Why, then, 'tis none to you; for there is nothing either good or bad, but thinking makes it so: to me it is a prison.

The idea Hamlet expressed was not new even in Shakespeare's day, but mirrored a scripture from Proverbs: "As a man thinks in his heart, so he is." (It all goes back to Shakespeare and the Bible, doesn't it?)

The power of thought and words has been studied extensively in psychology and medicine. The form of psychotherapy known as Cognitive Behavioral Therapy (CBT) has been successfully applied to a wide spectrum of ailments from back pain and anxiety to addictions and insomnia. At root, CBT aims to replace unhelpful thinking and behaviors with healthier beliefs.

In popular psychology and self-help, Expensive Sentences are not unlike "limiting beliefs" and "self-talk." Both of these labels reflect to the ideas that individuals adopt and rehearse, either in their mind or out loud. Identifying and changing the beliefs and resulting words has led to profound changes in many lives.

Breaking through Bias and Resistance

As we noted several times in this book, Expensive Sentences are closely connected to biases. You probably have a bias against bias; it's become a loaded word. But we all have biases, they are not necessarily bad, and in fact they are essential for the human brain to function. The best book I have encountered about cognitive biases is *Thinking, Fast and Slow* by Daniel Kahneman. His groundbreaking, Nobel-prize-winning research with Amos Tversky has opened up a new era of understanding how our brains work.

Kahneman and others present neuroscience; but there's more to us than just science. In his classic work on the creative process *The War of Art*, Steven Pressfield describes the concept of *resistance*. This topic is also explored brilliantly in *Linchpin* by Seth Godin. Resistance is not simply inertia or everyday challenges. It is personified as an active enemy whose purpose is to keep the individual from achieving the creative works they were created to do. It is our "lizard brain" which tells us to flee risk and achievement and instead stay small, safe, and silent.

Expensive Sentences are missiles of resistance, writ large across teams and organizations. Yes, we encounter our daily portion of excuses, inertia, politics and bureaucracy… and this book can be used as a field guide to cut through all of that banality. Yet in my mind, the origins of Expensive Sentences can be more sinister and their impact more destructive than simple inefficiencies and cost. My hope is that this book can stand with Pressfield's, Godin's, and others as an offensive weapon against resistance.

If you are interested in further reading, I strongly recommend each of the books noted in this section. I thank you for reading *Expensive Sentences*, and sincerely hope that it will pay rich dividends for you and your team.

ACKNOWLEDGMENTS

SOMETIMES IT SEEMS LIKE I RECEIVE MORE AFFIRMATION THAN ANYONE I know... and yet for an effort like this I need every ounce of it. While so many helped me on this journey, I want to single out a small cadre of vital friends: Mike Manion, Mark Joseph, Pat Ennis, and Brad Phillips. All of you consistently see more in me than I see in myself, and you believed that Expensive Sentences was a book that needed to be written.

If the book is useful, much of the credit goes to my outstanding editor Catherine Oliver.

My greatest encourager is my spectacular wife. Her abundant energy spurs me on, and her confidence in me is invaluable. I could never have done this without her. Yes, that's an Expensive Sentence, and it's absolutely true. Thank you Linda!

ENDNOTES

1   The quotes for Napoleon and the French Generals were taken from an English translation of the Count de Segur's 1824 narrative *Histoire de Napoleon et de la Grande Armee pendant l'annee 1812*, praised for its objectivity and accuracy by many who took part in the campaign. It's an excellent read.

2   The ski trip experiment about sunk costs was described in "The Psychology of Sunk Costs" by Harold R. Arkes and Catherine Blumer, Ohio University 1985.

3   Psalm 103:12 "He has removed our sins as far from us as the east is from the west." This wording is from the New Living Translation.

4   I learned the term "tyranny of the urgent" by reading Covey's *First Things First*, but its origin (as Covey rightly attributes) is a 31-page pamphlet by Charles Hummel titled… you guessed it: *Tyranny of the Urgent*.

5   Harry Chapin briefly explained the origins of the song "Cat's in the Cradle" at a live performance on Soundstage, and it was there he made the comment: "… and frankly, this song scares me to death."

6   There are many books that address delegation. One of the best is *E-myth Revisited* by Michael E. Gerber. Gerber describes business infancy as the phase when the business owner and the business are one in the same; this does not end until the owner learns to delegate.

7   The demand for home organization products is growing at roughly four percent annually, according to studies by the Freedonia group reported by Geometrx on April 11, 2013. Some categories, such as garage storage systems, are growing faster. When it comes to organizational services, demand is still greater. The success of Marie Kondo's books brought global focus on this field, and the growth of the National Association of Professional Organizers reveals its breadth. One of my heroes in this field is office organizer Kacy Paide, who sends out an excellent newsletter.

8   "Busyness addiction" is a subject that has produced numerous articles in psychology, lifestyle, and faith-related periodicals and websites. Two good ones are at the websites of Rands in Response and the Future Leadership Institute.

9   In the book *Dialogue in Organizations*, Megan Reitz presents her findings on how the pace and busyness level of many organizations are damaging communication and curtailing creativity. Dr. Reitz is on faculty at England's Ashbridge Business School.

10   Ian Altman writes and speaks about making sure you are talking to clients about "problems that are worth solving" in many places. Ian is a good friend and we authored *Same Side Selling* together; I highly recommend his teaching which you can find on his website *www.IanAltman.com*.

11   I've read many articles about FedEx and its history; in this case I relied on the company website's presentation of "our story."

12   I've come across the LATTE method in several articles, and most of those attribute learning it from Charles Duhigg, who described it in his outstanding book *The Power of Habit*.

13   Nearly every worthwhile business strategy book emphasizes the importance of differentiation. One of the most popular that I would recommend is *Different* by Youngme Moon. (Disclaimer: I have not yet read the full book.)

14   I still love Quiznos sandwiches, and I am rooting for the chain to recover. Because the fast food business is so visible–and because low franchise fees enticed many would-be entrepreneurs to open a Quiznos—the woes of the enterprise were widely chronicled. One of the best articles about Quiznos' challenges was published in Medium in March 3, 2014 by James Dasilva. Another is from the Denver Post on March 15, 2013 by Steve Raabe.

15   Southwest Airlines was the case-study darling when I went to Kellogg Business School in 1998-99, and my understanding is that they are still a favorite. There is an excellent, well-researched article on Ezine Articles website from December 11, 2005 that covers many facets of the company's success. A more recent article appeared in a blog on the Economist site June 18, 2012 that focuses on the airline's commitment to the 737.

16   This reference to Henry Ford's dry wit regarding the Model T underlines the prior section's message that uniformity reduces cost. It was the mass production of the Model T that brought the world into a new era of extremely efficient manufacturing, and also brought the age of the automobile by lowering the cost so that working people around the world could afford one. (In the same era, Ford doubled the wages for his factory workers, which led to widespread pay increases.) In case you haven't heard the quip, Henry Ford boasted that customers could get the Model T in "any color you want, so long as it's black."

17 Henry David Thoreau wrote the verse about "a different drummer" in *Walden*.

18 Ben Franklin printed the proverb "for want of a nail..." in *Poor Richard's Almanac*. It's possible that he was repeating it from somewhere else, but we'll give him credit since we can't possibly give Franklin too much credit.

19 Electronic Recruiting News, February 18, 2009: "Watson Wyatt's 2008/2009 WorkUSA Report found that when employees are highly engaged, their companies enjoy 26 percent higher employee productivity, have lower turnover risk and are more likely to attract top talent. Their companies have also earned 13 percent greater total returns to shareholders over the last five years." Later that year the company later merged with Towers Perrin to become Towers Watson. The company released another study in 2012, summarized by the Harvard Business Review in a November 8, 2012 article by Tony Schwartz. The 2012 study revealed a 10 percent operating margin for companies with low engagement, and a 27 percent margin for companies with the highest "sustainable engagement" scores.

20 I didn't invent "The Six Whys," and I'm not sure who did. (I'm guessing whoever it was had a four-year-old at home.) There is a similar exercise called "The Five Whys" in the Six Sigma toolkit used to determine root cause, and it's possible that the Six Whys is an adaptation of that.

21 Matthew 13:12 – the wording in the text is taken from the New International Version.

22 My favorite version of this quote from the great Julius Erving is: "When you're looking for daylight, daylight will be found." I believe I had a Dr. J poster with this wording on it 30 years ago, however I could not find the quote reproduced anywhere. The quote I use in the book is from an interview with the Academy of Achievement, posted in December 2007.

23 Jack Welch's famous approach to talent management is described in his book *Winning*, Chapter 7. This is an outstanding business management book, worth reading and re-reading.

24 I learned about Marshall Field and his stores first by visiting the flagship store in downtown Chicago in 1998, and was heartbroken when Macy's parent May Company decided not to preserve the brand after acquiring the chain in 2004. Field was one of the greatest retail innovators. You can learn more about him in many places, but most fittingly in the book *Give the Lady What She Wants: The Story of Marshall Field & Company* by Lloyd Wendt and Herman Kogan.

25 The phrase "only three things can happen when you throw the football, and two of them are bad" is most often attributed to Woody Hayes of Ohio State, but is also associated with Darrel Royal of the Texas Longhorns. It first appeared in print in 1963, and has been repeated by nearly every football broadcaster in the years since.

26 The Lego story is drawn from the 2013 book *Brick by Brick* by David C. Robertson. It's a great book about balancing company with growth and change, and is especially fun to read if you remember playing with the many Lego lines that are chronicled. (Which I do… though my younger brother Ben really hit the sweet spot with the mini-figures and the castle and space lines; good thing I had the excuse of getting sets for him.)

27   The HBR article "Defeating Feature Fatigue" sums up much of the research revealed in the 2006 study by the Harvard Business Review. It's interesting to reflect on that research now that we are well into the smartphone era.

28   I heard this story from a tour guide at the Frank Lloyd Wright home and studio in Chicago. I was not able to corroborate it anywhere, so it may be apocryphal. So I present it as a story and not history… it certainly is authentic to the spirit of Wright and other visionaries.

29   RCA anchored the dawn of the television age. The company's story is well told in the 2002 book *RCA* by Robert Sobel.

INDEX